Getting a
COLLEGE
DEGREE
Fast

Frontiers of Education

Series Editor: Ronald H. Stein, Ph.D.

(Complete Series Listing)

Getting a
COLLEGE DEGREE
Fast

Testing Out & Other
Accredited Short Cuts

Joanne Aber, Ph.D.

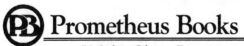
Prometheus Books

59 John Glenn Drive
Amherst, NewYork 14228-2197

Published 1996 by Prometheus Books

Inquiries should be addressed to
Prometheus Books, 59 John Glenn Drive, Amherst, New York 14228–2197.
VOICE: 716–691–0133, ext. 207. FAX: 716–564–2711.
WWW.PROMETHEUSBOOKS.COM

03 02 01 00 99   7 6 5 4 3

Library of Congress Cataloging-in-Publication Data

Aber, Joanne.
    Getting a college degree fast : testing out & other accredited short cuts / Joanne Aber.
        p.   cm.
    Includes index.
    ISBN 1–57392–001–0 (alk. paper)
    1. College-level examinations—United States. 2. College credits—United States—Outside work. 3. Experiential learning—United States. 4. Degrees, Academic—United States. I. Title.
LB2353.67.A34   1995
378.1'68'097—dc20   95–35979
                                                                          CIP

Printed in the United States of America on acid-free paper

Dedication

"All the flowers of all the tomorrows
are in the seeds of today."

Vera Hamscher Aber

To Bill and Daelyne for their unconditional love; and to Erik and Karen for sharing their outlook on life; to the memory of my parents, Vera and David, who were ahead of their time; Nancy and Basil Leschuk for their encouragement; and Regina C. Zuefle, who taught me that dreams come true.

Acknowledgments

My heartfelt appreciation to many dear friends and professional colleagues who cheered me on.

A special thank you to Steven L. Mitchell, my editor; and the adult education professionals who assisted me in providing the resources in this book, among them: Joan Schwartz, American Council on Education; Marcie Kisner Thorson, Thorson's Guides; Ruth Hendricks and staff at Educational Testing Service; Dr. David Lutz and staff at American College Testing; Dr. David Moffitt and staff at Ohio University Independent Study Program (CCE); Peterson's Guides; the staff at the Council for Adult and Experiential Learning (CAEL); Richard Pratt and Gail Veltman at the Wichita State University's Counseling and Testing Center; and the staffs at Regents College and Thomas Edison State College.

Contents

PART 2: NUTS AND BOLTS OF *TESTING OUT*

What People Like You Are Saying About Accredited Short Cuts

Getting a degree *fast* through the testing connection is simple once you know how to start. Here are just a few of the many enthusiastic comments I received after presenting the valuable step-by-step methods available to anyone who seeks an undergraduate degree.

"This information points you to the resources you need. It is very interesting and useful."

> Mary Lynn, a human
> services manager

"This is really good information. My technical program is being phased out at my community college, and the state college is not going to accept my credits for the degree I want. Now, I can look at other schools (off-campus/distance college degree programs) for my degree."

> Julie, 39, has 54 college credits in architecture

"This information has saved me a year's worth of research time finding these short cuts!"

> Bob, 35, manager of a food merchandise company, is a high school graduate with some college and some company training

"I am really excited! I need you to answer a few questions, so I can get started."

> Bernice, 50, a self-employed high school graduate with some college

"I really didn't know you could do this. I am interested in getting a bachelor's degree in engineering now."

> Ron, 48, a designer/drafts-man with an associate's degree

"This information is interesting, but I would have to check my education field to see how it applies. I liked learning about it. Some of it might apply to a degree for me. It gets old having my degreed co-workers act like I am less than them without one."

> Jeri, 44, a paraprofessional school tutor with one semester of college

"I dropped out of college to do consulting. Although I am financially successful, a degree would give me personal satisfaction. I can see the testing connection for me in computer-related subjects to complete my degree."

> Jeff, 29, a computer whiz with some college

"This information is good. It really can help. It excites me to think a degree could be accomplished this way."

> Val, 54 and mother of eight, a self-employed high school graduate

"This information has been interesting and I can see I need to get started on a graduate degree. I'm not getting any younger. I know my wife was thinking of adding to her nursing degree. This information can help her."

> Chet, 37, a manager with a college degree

"We have extensive company training that will help our executives achieve a degree. This information has been beneficial in identifying programs appropriate for our managers and saving us many hours of research."

> Marj, a human resource
> management professional

"My supervisor was promoted. I want to be promoted to her position. Having sixty credits, I can now finish my degree faster than I had thought possible."

> Lori, 37, a museum/theme
> park employee with two
> years of college

"This is really something. I'd like to talk to a counselor one-on-one about this."

> Tony, 38, an air condition-
> ing serviceman with high
> school and vocational
> diplomas

"This is exciting. I know I can finish faster than a traditional degree, but I plan to approach this traditionally, test-by-test (course-by-course), using off-campus degree work. I travel 50 percent of the time for my company, and can't consider a campus degree."

> Aggie, 42, division direc-
> tor of an international com-
> pany, and a high school
> graduate

"I write training manuals and will eventually need a degree for advancement."

> Tiya, 35, a training manager, and high school graduate

"I have professional certifications, yet company changes require department heads to have a bachelor's degree. I know independent study programs will work for me."

> Linda, 40, employed by an international food management organization, with between 60 and 90 college credits

"I train people who have degrees, and I don't. This information will really help me get started."

> Lisa, 32, publishing sales representative and telemarketer with a high school diploma

"This will be something I want to do before I'm forty. Thanks."

> Juanita, 34, an office worker and high school graduate

"I used your suggestions for testing and life credits assessment, and will be graduating from college in less than a year. I am thrilled!"

> Lee, 44, regional office manager for a national insurance company, with some college and many years of insurance training

"We're really excited that both my husband (a high school graduate in the military reserves, with courses through the military) and I can think about finishing our degrees."

> Marion, 27, an insurance clerk with over two years of college

"I am sending for the Regents books now!"

> Ed, 35, manager of a hardware store, with one semester of college sixteen years ago

Washington, Lincoln, Truman, and You

Did you know that presidents George Washington, Abraham Lincoln, and Harry Truman never went to college, yet they are among our best-known and most respected leaders? All three were avid self-taught, distance, and *independent study* learners of their time. None of these men had the high-tech learning resources that we now possess. In modern times, Truman has been the only president who lacked college training, but he had extensive experiential learning (lifelong learning) from his business career.

This raises an important point: the professional demands of today's business climate dictate the need for an undergraduate degree—"academic currency"—that can open the doors for most employment and facilitate advancement within a profession. Had Washington, Lincoln, or Truman been evaluated by the personnel departments of today's corporate employers, not one of them would have met most of the application requirements, and none would be interviewed, let alone hired! In the 1990s, like it or not, academic credentials have become the passport to the workplace. From all indications, this trend will continue into the foreseeable future.

In the past eight years some people attending my group sessions have said, "A degree doesn't mean you are smart and talented. I know many smart and talented people who do not have a degree." My reply: "Yes, I have, too. I used to be one of them."

Over the past two decades, more and more adults have returned to college to complete a degree. Those young college graduates, who gave rise to the stereotypical statement, "Some college graduates are really not too smart on the job," have acquired twenty years experience with their degree. It is counterproductive for today's adults to insist on burying their heads in the sand or saying that they can get through life without the "academic currency" their competition possesses.

DISTANCE EDUCATION REVISITED

The "new" trend toward learning methods such as distance education and *independent study* is not new in America. From the 1800s to just before World War II, rural towns lacked immediate access to the colleges in urban settings, so correspondence courses were designed and delivered to meet the course needs of these rural residents. Eventually these distance learning programs were available to the nation at large. From the mid-1800s to the early 1900s, Lyceums were developed by eastern colleges, sending speakers nationwide to cities and country towns to conduct lectures and thoughtful discussions on educational topics and new ideas for the average working class men and, yes, women.

If great leaders and everyday men and women of the past, most of whom lacked formal education, have learned in this way, think what you can do!

A Brief History of the Testing Connection and the Accelerated Degree Movement[*]

TESTING: A THUMBNAIL SKETCH

In 1992, the number of people who tested for course credit using the College Level Exam Program (CLEP) exceeded 200,000, and those using the American College Testing Proficiency Examination Program: Regents College Exams (PEP:RCE) numbered approximately 40,000. By 1994 the number of testers in CLEP was approximately 250,000, and those testing with PEP:RCE were over 65,000. Based on these figures and on the rate of growth each year, in just these two test-

---

*Information for this history was derived in part from an interview with Dr. Barbara Watkins from the University of Kansas, Division of Independent Study, and editor of *Foundations of American Distance Education* (1993); Susan Simisko and associates, from *Assessing Learning: A CAEL Handbook for Faculty* (1988); and testing statistics from both College Level Exam Program (CLEP) and the American College Testing Proficiency Examination Program: Regents College Examinations (PEP:RCE) materials.

ing programs, since 1970, a fair estimate would be that over five million tests have been taken. And the numbers keep growing each year.

These figures, coupled with the untold numbers from other nationally accepted testing systems and from departmental and challenge exams administered over the past twenty years, may well bring the number of tests taken to more than ten million. These systems, whose potential has yet to be tapped, reflect a substantial part of the academic credits achieved by college students of all ages for the past twenty-five years.

THE FIRST NATIONAL TEST

The Advanced Placement Program (APP) was the first college-level testing system developed by the College Board and administered by Educational Testing Service (ETS, 1955). Its primary purpose was to evaluate high school seniors for college-level proficiency in first-year college subjects. By 1963, the New York State Education Department developed the College Proficiency Examination Program, with the slogan, "What you know is more important than how you learned it." This program became nationally known as American College Testing Proficiency Examination Program: Regents College Examinations (PEP:RCE). These exams cover subjects in the first two years (the lower level), and some junior and senior (upper-level) subjects.

In 1965, the College Board developed the College Level Examination Program (CLEP), and over the years this testing system has become the most frequently used for credit-by-examination. These exams cover the first two years of (lower-level) college subjects.

Following CLEP, the Educational Testing Service provided Defense Activity for Non-Traditional Educational Support (DANTES), tests originally developed for the military. In recent years these tests have been made available to the public at large.

Together, CLEP/DANTES, PEP:RCE, and APP provide over 150 standardized subject exams in the arts, business, computer science, education, science, nursing, and technical and occupational areas.

THE ACCELERATED DEGREE MOVEMENT

Accelerated degrees evolved, in part, as a result of accredited short cuts. As we have seen, these short cuts were developed by education services like ETS and by various American colleges. Two additional reasons for the rapid growth of accelerated degree programs were the rising cost of a degree during the post–World War II period and the need for a more specialized work force.

In addition, gifted education programs, many of which began in kindergarten and developed through the elementary and secondary schools, meant that by the time some students graduated from high school they were academically prepared to start at the sophomore year of college. The APP was developed to verify this academic achievement.

Changes in the way educators viewed adults proved the final wave of development in the accelerated degree (AD) movement. Colleges met the needs of adult students by creating the original extension course and the correspondence course as well as developing and implementing college-level exams and the external degree. Private colleges, in both their broader mission to serve adults returning to college and their need to tap a market, were front runners in the development of ADs by creating degree completion programs that accepted a combination of prior learning and credits earned from the college for the final year of a degree ("one year to a college degree").

Accelerated degrees featuring portfolio assessment became a boon to adults returning to school even though there were skeptics within the academic community. The general consensus among academics is that the first well-known accelerated adult degree program was initiated in the early seventies by the College of New Resources at the College of New Rochelle, a private Catholic institution. Later, adult degree learning began at outreach sites off campus in and around the New York City area. From what I have read and heard, these programs were originally for students who could afford to attend class if they desired, but later the programs evolved to serve economically disadvantaged and working-class adult students.

Preface

The Testing Connection

> "Don't wait for your ship to
> come in. Swim out after it."
>
> Unknown

When I turned forty I said, "I need a degree yesterday!" Do you feel this way? Do you feel left out of the employment market? Do you have forgotten dreams? Do you have silent fears about your future without a degree? Have you thought that a degree could or would have made the difference in your life? Have you thought that a degree was impossible for someone your age, with your income, and with your family responsibilities?

If you answered yes to one or more of these questions, then this book can help you get a degree *fast*.

LET'S TALK

As this book was developing it became clear that to be effective and helpful, it would have to be a conversation between you, the reader, and me. We will discuss *testing out* and accredited short cuts, but also how to get a degree *fast* and on your own terms.

As an adult you have general knowledge about college degrees. You may even have knowledge of the basic steps you would take to complete a degree. With this book and a little determination, you can develop an operational knowledge about today's college degrees and the short cuts available at *all* colleges to help you *chart your course* to the degree *you* want.

DON'T BE DISMISSED

By the time I was forty-one, regardless of my successes, I realized I had little or no access to employment, no likelihood of advancement when I was employed, and no career opportunities (what some call upward mobility).

> In 1986, at one nonprofit agency, the president told me that even though my accomplishments were well known to their organization, and to him personally, the position I was applying for required an undergraduate degree. Since I did not have one, he said he did not have to accept my application. As I look back, I am not sure he even asked if I had a degree. He assumed I didn't. Not having one, I bought into his dismissal.
>
> I was angry. I felt like I had been drop-kicked. "If they (the world at large) want a piece of paper, I'll give them a piece of paper." Determined to get around this brick wall, I remembered my college-level testing and quickly learned everything I could about accelerated learning methods, and soon began a marathon of testing for college credit, taking two and three tests per month.

After this experience and hearing statements like "If you had a degree, you would have better employment opportunities" one too many times, I was driven to do "whatever it takes" to complete a college degree.

Even as angry as these experiences made me, a funny thing happened on the way to my associate's degree. I began to love learning for learning's sake!

FAST-TRACK METHODS TO A DEGREE

Ultimately, I used fast-track methods including *testing out,* to earn *all but ten credits* for an associate's and a bachelor's degree, attending for a third of a master's degree and completing a doctorate, in less than seven and a half years. In that time, through my own degree path and eventually as an adult education consultant, I discovered the variety of testing systems available for students of all ages, and related "accredited short cuts" that can speed the degree process, especially for adults over the age of thirty.

DEGREES ARE SIMPLIFIED BUT NOT SIMPLE

Since the 1970s, these accredited short cuts have been used by millions of students, many of whom are over the age of thirty, to meet their dream of achieving an undergraduate degree. I will "walk" you through the many available resources, describe an array of short cuts that exist today (innovative approaches that continue to grow in number and develop year after year), and share the story of my degree path along the way.

As you think about what you want out of life and how a degree can help you reach your goals, remember, in the nineties, these short cuts are multifaceted, comprehensive, and able to accommodate the adult learner. They can help you simplify the way you complete a degree.

Rest assured that the short cuts you will read about in this book do not "short sheet" the college system. Instead, they expedite it. *Testing out,* accredited short cuts, and accelerated degrees were developed by colleges as part of their educational service to the public they are entrusted to serve.

ALL COLLEGE CREDITS REQUIRE COLLEGE-LEVEL LEARNING

Since life is a learning process, no doubt you have accumulated a lifetime of learning (some of which might be college-level) in the years since high school. You may have knowledge through your hard work and effort in your private and public life that can be credentialized through short cuts to help you achieve a degree faster.

BIG BUSINESS

Enticing adults to return to college is big business. Be cautious about the variety of media hype you hear and read; many times it is paid for by colleges and contains degree promos and promises on television, radio, and billboards, and in magazines and newspapers. These promotional campaigns may promise convenience, fewer classroom hours, and learning in a more mature setting, *but you still have to attend class*—and this is something many hard-working, accomplished adults just don't want to do.

WHAT CAN A COLLEGE DO FOR YOU?

It's a buyer's market; shop for the best degree package you can get. Remember, you are the consumer. As one of my learned colleagues has said many times, you have a right to the education you want, not what a college tells you it has decided to give you. This country was founded on the rights of the individual, yet colleges for the most part continue to have a take-it-or-leave-it attitude. With *testing out* and related short cuts you can overcome this limited business practice by picking and choosing the school you want and the degree program best suited to your needs.

THE TESTING CONNECTION

Testing out is your degree connection (accredited short cut): it's inexpensive and can be done almost totally at home, at minimal cost for books if you don't mind using the library. In what follows I have tried to give you a written guide through the maze of available college information. You will be pleasantly surprised to learn about the hundreds of subjects available to you through these short cuts. Remember: Education is a very personal matter. How, where, and when you get your education is not as important as your attitude and growth along the way.

Walk in sunshine,

Joanne Aber, Ph.D.
Adult and Continuing
Education Administration
Education Options
Wichita, Kansas

Introduction

The Lighter Side of a Degree

"Laughter is the course of all conversation."

Anonymous

I have two reasons for thinking of accelerated degrees using accredited short cuts as the lighter side of a degree. First, a degree can be accomplished without all the heavy, burdensome, traditional degree methods. Second, there are humorous, light-hearted moments along the way to any degree, but most especially the degrees completed by adults over the age of thirty. If, after reading this book, you decide to go back to college, you, too, will find that your thoughts of hard work will be replaced by accommodating degree programs and some well-deserved laughter along the way.[1] Trust me.

---

1. For the purposes of our discussion, the term "college" is used as a general term to mean both colleges and universities.

WHYS AND WHEREFORES

To understand and appreciate the whys and wherefores of *testing out*[2] and accredited short cuts (ASCs),[3] you need to know about accelerated degrees (ADs).[4] *Accelerated degrees* is an umbrella term, recognized by colleges, which refers to the method of completing a degree by accelerating the process of college-level learning. In other words, even if some classroom attendance is required, a degree can be achieved without taking the traditional campus degree which incorporates a classroom-oriented approach based on the semester or quarter system.

In addition, ADs are further defined by their delivery system, which provides opportunities to shorten the time spent on required course work. This degree completion[5] method incorporates *testing out* to take advantage of prior learning. In contrast to a traditional degree, ADs can be achieved and granted without the constraints of campus residency requirements[6] or administrative paperwork (bureaucracy).

---

2. "Testing out" refers to college-level testing that is accepted at most colleges in place of course-by-course credits. They are explained more fully throughout this book, and in the section titled "Terms You Need to Know."

3. "Accredited short cuts" is a term that refers to all methods of college-level learning that do not require campus attendance.

4. "Accelerated degrees" refers to degrees that are established to speed up the college process for adult learners.

5. "Degree completion" refers to any degree program that assists adults over the age of twenty-five to complete a college degree.

6. "Residency requirements" are the number of college credits required to be taken at the college from which you want your degree conferred.

YOU ARE UNIQUE

You are a special individual, yet you have probably had life experiences similar to those most adults have had in their private and public lives. My experiences included putting my family first rather than pursuing my education and career dreams. This meant taking any job available to help support my family, having to turn down jobs or experience unemployment due to family circumstances, and being able to secure only part-time employment for several years at a time. Occasionally these workplace experiences put a real dent in my self-esteem. My lack of access to and equity in the workplace was due in large measure to being without an undergraduate degree.

In the early 1960s, after high school graduation, I planned to attend vocational school full-time and college part-time. For me the funds for full-time degrees were not available, nor was there financial aid for part-time students.[7] After I earned my vocational diploma and was working, the high cost of a college education forced me to put my thoughts of a degree aside. I thought it was something that wouldn't happen in my lifetime.

I worked as a hairdresser in the late sixties and throughout the seventies, and as far as I knew colleges made little effort to attract, let alone accommodate, the degree needs of adult students. In my mid-thirties my health changed, making it impossible to work at hairdressing, so I began to work in offices and retail. As a hairdresser, degrees were not required. In the office and retail world, it was made abundantly clear that I would not be a valued employee without one.

I was stunned. I had "bought" into the American myth of my generation of women: we were to marry, raise our children and meet family obligations, do volunteer work, and when all that had been dutifully accomplished, we would be welcomed into the workplace

---

7. Financial aid for part-time students is just now (1995) being considered by Congress.

with access and equity that included dignity and advancement. Our valuable life experiences would be accepted in place of a degree. Well, the joke was on me, and many other women (men, too), because I believed the hype doled out in women's magazines, at women's support groups, and career seminars (many were government funded) that fostered this philosophy. I woke up at forty and said to myself, and anyone who would listen, "What a lie!"

Reality began to set in. I had lost "ground" by following my husband from one military transfer to another, including three years in Panama. After my divorce and remarriage to a civilian (who had job changes that crisscrossed the country), I concentrated on raising my children, handling complicated custody issues (which dragged on for five years after my divorce), and helped change a few domestic court laws along the way. I volunteered as a community service worker for major charities, took on the responsibility for the eldercare of my parents and my husband's parents, and worked for any employer who would hire me. Through it all I kept hitting an imaginary brick wall: no amount of private and public experience or "networking" (a buzz word that has been used as the cure-all for problems related to employment opportunities in the eighties and nineties) would ever lead me to employment that paid much more than minimum wage. When I wasn't working for others, I owned a twelve-operator beauty salon and an advertising consulting business, but the profits from these ventures did not support (or help support) a family.

It was clear that without a degree, meaningful employment leading to economic advancement would not be possible. In fact, as I mentioned earlier, one nonprofit organization wouldn't even allow me to fill out a job application unless I had a degree!

But each and every time the thought of a degree surfaced, I would ignore it, find another deadend job, and go on with my life. By the age of forty, the thought of a degree began to hang over my head like a cloud. No amount of rationalizing would make it go away. As a mother with economic constraints, the affordability of a degree still seemed impossible. Even ADs with claims of flexibility in both time and money continued to seem a remote possibility.

In 1982, I had tested for eighteen college credits at the suggestion of a college professor I met while doing political volunteer work. My first College Level Exam Program (CLEP) test was English Composition. My first test score—A! After that, I was pretty smug and took three more CLEPs.

During the mid-eighties, I continued to check on various ADs, the ones that claimed "one year to a college degree." But none of these degree programs would work for me. To qualify I needed two years of college course work (a minimum of sixty credits), to which I could then earn a "year's worth" of credits (thirty) from life experience inside the degree completion program. My life seemed like the flip side of those requirements. Once again, I put a degree on the "back burner."

In 1985, I actually went to a college offering an accelerated degree to hear its free information session. An admissions counselor reviewed my prior education and the college generously offered to allow 12 science credits from my vocational training[8] plus any of my 1982 testing credits. In fact, this school had no limits on testing credits up to the first 90, as long as the credits met its degree requirements. In my case, I could test out for the first 78 credits to meet my need for prior college credits to add to my 12 science credits for a total of 90. I could then attend college for that "final year" in its degree completion program.

8. This was before many vocational schools and colleges had worked together on cooperative agreements to accomplish two- and four-year degrees.

WAIT NO MORE: MY FIRST CAMPUS CLASS

In 1986, twenty-two years after high school, with the foundation of those eighteen testing credits, I could wait no longer. My formal college career gathered steam when I wrote a paper for college credit after attending a professional workshop offered at a private college, and attended a state college for my first official college course on entrepreneurship.[9]

When I took my first college course on campus, I was anything but well prepared for the world of college. In fact, the beginning of my college attendance was almost the end of my academic career.

It was a three-week summer course taught on campus with day and night sessions. It accommodated two hundred students of all ages (including traditional students under age twenty-five) in a large auditorium. It featured speakers who were successful entrepreneurs (some famous) including the founders of Residence Inns, Rent-A-Center, and several Pizza Hut franchise directors.

The first day of the class, as I stood up to the microphone to ask a question of that day's guest entrepreneur, I made comments about my national connections to entrepreneurs they had mentioned in the lecture, and then asked my question. As I left the class, I felt negative vibes from the professor and felt uncomfortable around the other students. When I arrived home, I felt like a child on the first day of kindergarten, swallowed up by two hundred classmates. I declared that I was not going back. My husband was supportive: "You probably know more than most people in the class and you owe it to yourself to go back."

So back I went the second day. When it came time for the question and answer session, I stood up once again to await my turn at the microphone. The professor came up behind me, unannounced, and

---

9. Wichita State University, Wichita, Kansas, presented this course.

told me to "stick to the subject of the class," whatever that meant. So I asked my question and went home, vowing to drop the course.

Again, my husband, now joined by my children, insisted that I go back. I did. Still, I continued to feel uncomfortable, and I came home determined to transfer to the night session of the same class, to see if it was different.

When I called the daytime professor to transfer, he apologized to me, and gave me what I now call academic "schmoozing." He asked me to stay in the daytime class, since they needed "creative questions" like mine (!?!), to stimulate the class. I stayed. The rest, as they say, is history.

While taking this business course, I realized how much life's lessons had taught me. As I completed this campus course, my confidence returned and I once again started testing for credit. I was on a wave of success and nothing could stop me!

FROM EIGHTEEN CREDITS TO A DOCTORATE

As an avid reader, I was confident that I knew a sizable amount of college-level subject material, and I was determined to achieve the degree that would be the key to professional success.

My college-level testing began with a vengeance. From May to September, taking three tests each month, I passed college-level tests for thirty-one undergraduate credits. With the three credits from the campus course, one from the workshop, and eighteen credits from prior testing, I had accumulated fifty-three college credits. From that point on, I continued to test my way to an associate of science degree, with a concentration in human resource management, and a bachelor of science degree with dual majors in political science and sociology.

It was during this first year of my serious college work that a business acquaintance said to me over lunch, "I've seen many talented women, and men, get nowhere in business without a degree. If there is any way you can see your way to get a degree, you should do it." Originally, my intent was just to credentialize my lifelong learning[10] without actually seeking the degree. But comments like this encouraged me greatly. At this early stage on my road to a degree something unexpected happened: my thirst for deeper learning began to blossom. I no longer wanted to "just get by." I wanted more than a piece of paper saying I had a degree. This passion for college-level learning has continued through to my doctorate and beyond.

My two undergraduate degrees, which I completed almost entirely off campus, opened up opportunities for me to attend graduate school and to teach college. And all of my degrees are *accredited degrees*. None are from diploma mills.

Before you read on, let's discuss diploma mills. These are illegal, mail-order businesses often with names similar to known colleges. In return for a fee those who answer ads are sent a piece of paper that looks very much like a diploma containing all the usual college degree language. Most diploma mills are backroom operations that are not sanctioned by any regional accrediting agency. Their degrees lack substance and are literally not worth the paper they are written on.

Many good accredited degree programs exist and are serving adults both nationally and internationally. This means that there are legitimate accelerated degree programs for any adult who is serious about degree completion. With so many accredited programs available, why would anyone even consider a diploma mill? Take my advice, avoid them! If you are not sure about a particular school, check the institution by inquiring with an accrediting agency.

---

10. "Lifelong learning" refers to learning, both formal and informal, from all parts of an individual's life.

HELPING OTHER ADULTS

As my degree path moved forward rapidly, my excitement was boundless. Business and academic colleagues encouraged me to start an educational consulting business that would provide information about accredited short cuts (ASCs) to others who had an interest in getting a degree *fast.* In addition to my own interest in ASCs, and requests from clients while *testing out,* I discovered there where many more accelerated degrees and learning methods in addition to the few I was using. In fact, there are as many combinations for degree completion as there are adults over thirty seeking and completing undergraduate degrees.[11]

When I conduct group and individual presentations, the feedback is overwhelmingly positive from participants, who begin to see a connection between accomplishing college credits with one tested subject to completion of an entire degree program through *testing out* or a combination of ASCs. What they see is access to the immediate starting points. When the limitations imposed on adults by traditional college thinking are lifted, their potential is unlimited.

ALL COLLEGES BEING EQUAL

There are over ten thousand colleges in the United States; some better, some that are not as good. With a large percentage of these colleges offering accelerated degrees (ADs) in response to the many adults who want a college education, you need to realize that these schools and the ADs they confer are no better or worse than any traditional degree path you could choose. If you believe that only a big-

---

11. It should be noted here that undergraduate degrees for students up to age twenty-five are covered by traditional programs as well as grants and student loans. For students over age sixty, most state college systems provide free classes or reduced-cost courses.

name college will do, then you have created some self-imposed limitations. If you have no such limitations, you can progress as fast as you want to complete your degree.

If you need a degree *as fast as possible,* you can consider any college, anywhere, that allows accelerated methods of degree completion. However, if you have an "academic currency" requirement—meaning that the degree or diploma you earn at a specific institution or select group of institutions is preferred by the profession you plan to enter—then you must be cautious to locate *the* college that provides this currency.

ACADEMIC CURRENCY

My own skepticism and that of others regarding ADs, and hiring practices in the eighties, made me look at what I have dubbed "academic currency." It is common knowledge that preferred colleges exist for medicine, law, and science. Less prestigious professions carry some of this baggage with them as well, e.g., engineering, paralegal training, healthcare professions, and others. If you are in a profession that expects its members to graduate from a certain college or group of colleges, you need to address this in your planning for a degree.

Taking another example, at the local level, many employers prefer to hire "homegrown" workers. If this is true in your area of study or your geographic region, then using off-campus or other ADs from outside your area could be unwelcome when your resume is reviewed. Why waste your time and money seeking a degree from outside the preferred area when one of the local schools will make your degree more attractive to prospective area employers?

You owe it to yourself to complete a degree from the preferred college(s). You can still consider ASCs even with preferred colleges, and you can accelerate your degree process at the same time.

ON THE LIGHTER SIDE

Reaching your degree goals is very serious business, yet over the years my journey toward a college degree has had some humorous twists and turns. One thought struck me as I finished my doctorate: All of my academic work and study was conducted primarily at home (Kitchen Kollege), or at my favorite beach (Beach Basics). And, yet, when I attend meetings with other professionals at the doctoral level, for the most part we talk the same language.

This is not said to be disrespectful of the Ivy League or of academia in general. But one wonders: If students who use the many accredited home-based programs can effectively educate themselves, thereby meeting accredited, academic criteria, what's all the fuss been about? Where is it written that a big-name college, or any campus college with rectangular classrooms, teachers, course-by-course lessons, and midterm and final examinations, is the only avenue an individual should use to complete a college degree?

In 1990, as a colleague listened to a brief presentation I gave on my degree path and how these methods can be used by all college students, he commented: "The way you got your degrees is an indictment of the campus system as we know it. If you can arrive at this point (i.e., Ph.D. candidate), without attending campus classes, and you have the academic preparedness to begin a doctorate, basically from *independent study*,[12] what does this say about our campus system?" My response: "Adult learners can use these short cuts to their advantage." Respected colleges we hold in high regard developed these ASCs; for example, the College of New Resources at the

---

12. "Independent study" refers to any college coursework or required learning that is done away from campus. It can be done solely by itself without a degree program or as part of a degree program through a college or an external/distance degree program. It also refers to college-level learning completed on your own schedule, at your own pace, e.g., college-level testing, correspondence courses, and self-designed courses offered through colleges on or off campus.

College of New Rochelle, the Pennsylvania State University, Syracuse University, the University of New York (Regents College), and the New Jersey State College system (Thomas Edison State College), to name a few.

COLLEGE IN THE 1990s

Colleges in the nineties encourage, facilitate, and even welcome the adult learner on campus. However, occasionally there still tends to be some public disbelief, sometimes an unexplained suspicion, that some of the ADs and ASCs do not have the academic content and integrity of traditional campus coursework and degrees. For the most part, colleges seem to have overcome this resistance, perhaps because adult degree programs are such big business.

Still, colleges do not let a student go unbridled, wandering about without direction and guidance. Nor do they openly assist a student in finding ways to "design a degree."[13] You must know what you need and what you want in the way of a degree before you can achieve the best degree for you—*fast*.

Fast or slow, it's your choice. Do you want to move fast to complete a degree? Or do you prefer to move slowly through the college process? Either approach is okay. It's up to you.

In part 1 of this book you will discover what you need to get started on your degree path, and what others have done to complete their degrees. In part 2 you will be acquainted with testing systems by subject listing as well as colleges that accept testing as part of degree completion or as an accelerated degree path. In addition, part 2 includes a select bibliography of "Books You Should Read," a glossary of "Terms You Need to Know," a Mini-Quiz for Academic

---

13. "Design a degree" refers to your ability to use the many college systems available to you to complete a degree that reflects your personal lifelong learning (see chapter 1).

Preparation and Assessment, a College Check List, an outline of college tests I took while progressing toward my degree, and the addresses of college-level testing systems and accreditation agencies.

DREAM AND TAKE ACTION

As adults we tend to lose the dreams of our youth. Dreams fall away as we face economic, academic, and emotional and learning barriers that sometimes continue throughout our lives. Some of us fulfill our dreams, while others survive by holding on to the practical and reachable goals at the time. This brings me to a question I ask many people.

If you could turn back time to the days of high school, with no economic restrictions and/or learning barriers, where would you have gone to college and what would you have become?

When I asked myself this question a flood of "forgotten dreams" bubbled to the surface. Over the years, in some areas of my private and public life, I had realized some of my dreams. Still, for the most part, until my bachelor's degree was completed, my real dreams (deferred until my forties) were not realized.

As you read on, perhaps your forgotten dreams will surface and thoughts of pursuing a college degree, maybe from a prestigious, big-name college, will come to mind. After you revisit your dreams, you may experience a shock of reality, just as you did years ago. You come back to where you are recognizing that your dreams were sidelined and that you had to go on living your life. Delay no longer. While acceptance by a high-visibility, nationally recognized college may or may not be possible, the testing connection can certainly help you achieve your dream of earning a college degree!

ACCEPT NO LIMITATIONS

A degree, job advancement, and personal growth and satisfaction are just a few goals and objectives that can be reached with accredited short cuts. In the years since 1987, when my seminars and workshops began, it has continued to amaze me that accomplished, successful adults are turned off or frightened by dry educational readings and pronouncements. Knowing this, my goal will be to make this information come alive for you, and help you complete a degree in the *least amount of time* for the *least amount of money.*

More and more publications are available on degree completion methods. I continue to find excellent programs and suggestions on how adults can get a degree on their own terms. While many degree programs are facilitating, they still have a higher price tag than *testing out.* All the publications I have read were helpful to me in finding focus for the two accelerated degrees I earned (see "Books You Should Read"). Once I learned about these methods, especially the freedom of testing and its affordability, I took action and accomplished my degree goals.

It is up to you to decide if accomplishing a degree using ASCs is right for you. If so, you will find learning about your degree options (a study in itself) to be a test of your self-directedness and determination to succeed. In the end it will enhance the degree process itself. This enhancement is self-affirming and as important to your learning as the subjects that yield a degree.

It's almost the year 2000. As this decade draws to a close and colleges approach the twenty-first century, they appear to appreciate their accelerated degree offerings, as do personnel directors or human resource managers at most companies. The public is much more aware as well. Frankly, every major metropolitan college offers some form of accelerated degrees. From now on, the world is your oyster!

The bottom line—*testing out* and ASCs are inexpensive and they worked for me. They can work for you, too! *Accept no limitations!*

Part One

It Can Be Done!

"The mind, once stretched by a new idea, never regains its original dimension."

Oliver Wendell Holmes

1

Design a Degree

"An individual can succeed at almost anything with unlimited enthusiasm."

Charles Schwab

When you *design a degree*, you can start *anywhere*, with *any college*. However, I have found that if you first focus on the testing connection and related short cuts and how they can benefit your degree path, most of the operational knowledge of degree concepts you need to shape your degree will become clearer.

When you have completed this process of deciding which tests and other ASCs could work for you, you may reach the conclusion that a campus degree program is the right approach for you. But whatever you choose, you will be more self-directed and you will know what you want from each college you evaluate. *Most importantly* you will not leave your education in the hands of strangers!

HOW DID *DESIGN YOUR DEGREE* HAPPEN?

During the time it took me to begin my associate's degree and finish my bachelor's degree, while giving public presentations and writing articles on ADs and ASCs, I discovered individualized correspondence courses off campus, as well as on-campus *independent study* courses.

Further, my survey of the National University and College Education Association's top seventy-two colleges that provide correspondence courses,[1] revealed that there were "Problems Courses" offered at the University of Missouri (Columbia), a traditional campus college, through its correspondence department. These *independent study* courses, which can be structured for on-campus as well as off-campus students, can be developed for each individual in subjects that fall within the range of an academic department. They are usually taken in conjunction with a degree program, but can be taken on an individual basis as an open student.[2]

Additionally, I noticed the Ohio University's Lifelong Learning Programs had College Credit by Examination (CCE), correspondence courses, and independent study projects. This system provides a set group of subjects available for testing and *independent study* courses, as well as *individualized testing* and *correspondence* courses. Students can submit requests in *almost* all subjects available in the Ohio University system except lab courses (language, math, science, or technical). In addition, many colleges have departmental exams to evaluate a student's proficiency in a subject area, and many also grant *life credits*—credits for life experience with portfolio as-

---

1. Correspondence courses from accredited colleges provide campus content instructions through the mail. These courses usually do not require being registered at any college. Some require prerequisites (prior courses) to enroll. These are more fully discussed in the rest of the book.

2. Open students attend college on or off campus without being formally registered in a degree program.

sessment[3] (complete information about each of these will be provided later in the book).

In designing a degree, college-level testing for my major and minor area of concentration for my two undergraduate degrees reflected my lifelong learning. As an adult education consultant, learning about the many custom-designed educational options, including testing systems, was an "ah-ha" experience for me. This means that anyone who chooses ADs and uses ASCs can *design a degree*.

In addition, some colleges enter into learning agreements[4] with a student and develop study plans[5] in any academically accepted field of study. These learning agreements and study plans may include some or all of the above-mentioned ASCs, e.g., "problems courses" and individualized testing and correspondence courses. Their use results in unique, almost customized degrees unlike anyone else's.

DEGREES OF THE PAST AND FUTURE

If you are over thirty and never attended college, or attended but did not complete a degree, you probably have a vision or memories of college being formidable. And in the past most degrees were strictly academic, having little workplace relevance except for those pursu-

---

3. "Portfolio assessment" is a term that colleges use to describe the process that documents experiential learning from a student's life experiences and readings. These portfolios are usually governed and outlined by each individual college: each student must be aware of the specific requirements of a particular college before deciding if a portfolio assessment will reflect his or her experiential learning and assist in designing a degree.

4. "Learning agreement" refers to the contract that students make with a college to outline the courses they plan to use to complete a degree. These agreements are most often used with off-campus degrees.

5. "Study plan" refers to the planned learning a student does to complete a degree. These can be official, through a college, or informal and personal, as a guide for the learner. Study plans are usually used with off-campus degrees.

ing medical, nursing, legal, technical, or teaching degrees. Long registration lines that snaked around buildings were all too common. Entrance requirements included high SAT or ACT scores, entrance exams, along with a distinguished high school academic record. All this took money, lots of money.

COURSE BY COURSE, HOMEWORK, EXAMS

Many adults face these images of what college was (and remains in some degree programs) with considerable trepidation. The thought of long hours spent away from work and family, compounded by the tedium of rigid course schedules with cumbersome homework and exams stops many from pursuing degree completion. *Testing out*, ASCs, and ADs can change this view.

Accelerated degrees can accommodate adults, but the fees for attending that final "one year to a degree" can be as much as ten thousand dollars. The courses, or *modules*,[6] as they are called in many adult degree completion programs, still involve homework, reports, and attending classes, even if it is only *one day or night a week*. The difference with modules is that a student can concentrate on one or two subjects at a time.

Affordability may be a concern you face, as it was for me. There are low-cost ways to get a degree; you just have to search for them.

---

6. Modules are coursework designed to cover one subject at a time for adult degree completion programs based on the educational philosophy (grounded in adult education research) that adults with full schedules learn more efficiently one course at a time versus simultaneously taking a combination of courses.

CAREER: A NICE WORD FOR A JOB

Before any degree program is begun, a serious career assessment should be done. Before and during my college search, I included career assessment. I met with career counselors, read career assessment materials, talked with professionals in the career areas I wanted to be in, and read job opening notices and ads to zero in on the academic requirements, skills, and experiences needed.

Some colleges offer career assessment courses for one to three college credits (a way to start or add credits while assessing your career needs), while others provide them on a noncredit basis. You know your current profession better than anyone, or at least you have a considerable amount of knowledge about a career you want to enter. When you decide that your present career needs upward mobility or a complete change, there are four areas that require formal assessment. Ask yourself:

What formal credentials are required?

What formal credentials do I possess?

What formal credentials must be acquired?

What work experience do I have that will assist
in my upward mobility or career change?

Before you start any college program, it's well worth your time to check with career counselors, attend career seminars, read career guidance books and materials, and seriously consider career testing. Career assessments reveal details about your abilities (some you may not know you have) in relation to your present career or the career you hope to enter, and the required degree or adult education needed. Your local YMCA, YWCA, state employment centers, and most colleges have these services readily available. Some career guidance can even

be found in the programs and printed materials of the professional organizations related to your career choice.

Recently an individual told me that my general career assessment
information was not "specific enough and all telling." She felt I
should provide her with specific information on where to go to begin
a career assessment. This gave me pause for thought. If you are not
self-directed, with an inquiring mind and some sense of where you
would go for your personal career assessment, *perhaps ADs using
ASCs are not for you.* If so, this is the time to *stop* and do some serious soul searching. Take a good look at your motivation and your
determination.

While education for education's sake is never wasted, most of us
usually have limited time and financial resources. Aside from the fact
that so many excellent programs are accommodating the academic
needs and desires of adults, false starts and misdirected efforts are
unnecessary and frustrating. You don't need the aggravation. Be
smart. Get focused.

REALITY CHECK: DOES YOUR CAREER REALLY NEED A DEGREE?

At this point in our conversation, its worth noting that *not every career requires a college degree.* This might be contrary to the hype
you receive from the media and employment counselors, but a "reality check" belongs in a career assessment. Many careers do require
a degree, but many others do not. Depending on the profession, you
might need only a few brush-up courses, an associate's degree that
is technology-based, or just some technical training. Many well-
paid jobs do not require a bachelor's degree.

ACADEMIC SUCCESS AND FAILURE

As you complete your career assessment, you need to look at your academic history. Have you felt that academic failures, no matter how minor, have kept you from going to college? If this is true, let's look at how adult education in the nineties is delivered to adults. But before we do, let's look back before 1970. Most learning deficits[7] went undiagnosed and unaided. After 1970, these deficits were recognized and in most cases students were assisted in overcoming them from kindergarten through twelfth grade.

In addition to better educational methods of addressing learning deficits in children, adult educators began to match teaching and learning styles for optimum educational outcomes for their students. This means that adult students can take advantage of these innovations in education by identifying their learning preferences, e.g., lectures, videos, television, computer-aided learning, reading, and the like.

What does this mean to you? You can put your fears of academic failure aside. Your success in the workplace and in other areas of your life show that you may have overcome the issues that led to any lack of academic success. This success, and your added maturity, combined with a strong desire to achieve your goals can and usually do make the difference in your academic success as an adult student.

Academic Assessment: Reading and Math Help

Should you still have concerns, most local colleges have academic assessment and evaluations in reading and math to let you know your level of college preparedness. If you have reading and/or math deficits, colleges have remedial reading and math classes to assist

---

7. "Learning deficits" refers to the difficulty some individuals have with acquiring reading and math skills.

you on a noncredit or one-credit basis. They serve as an excellent way to get back to college and sharpen your skills.

Cold Sweats?

Speaking of sharpening your skills, are you breaking out in cold sweats over studying again after all these years? I will not try to "schmooze" you. It takes effort to get into the study mode for college no matter what your age. But there is good news. Once again, your workplace discipline and personal maturity will help you overcome this obstacle. And, in addition to remedial reading and math courses, most local colleges have courses on effective study techniques. These courses cover effective reading, how to take notes, and even how to overcome test fright.

Before we go on with our discussion, I would like to recommend Bill Bittel's sixty-two-page book *Adult Learners Survival Skills*.[8] This book will give you learning tips that any adult can use. This *little* book can make a *big* contribution to your academic success.

MY EDUCATIONAL BACKGROUND

Now that we have discussed career and academic assessment and the support services you can use, let's use my education path as an example of how to proceed. You may see yourself in some of my story.

After high school, my first postsecondary education was a vocational diploma in hairdressing. During high school (before the days of vocational or technical courses through high school) I attended summer classes and finished four months after my high school graduation. When I was a teenager my family struggled economically, and my mother was the sole provider by the time I grad-

---

8. Melbourne, Fla.: Kreiger Publishing Company, 1990.

uated from high school. Even so, back in the 1960s, much of the financial support for low-income college students either did not exist or the knowledge of such assistance was not made known to me.

The high school I attended favored college prep. For those of us whose families could not pay at least half of the projected college costs, regardless of solid academic backgrounds and good SAT scores, we were not given support or encouragement from guidance counselors to go to college. Unlike today, the two-year colleges of my youth were not as accepted or promoted as a substantial part of a four-year college effort.

Vocational training was my choice. Even at that my family was barely able to afford it. My mother, a registered nurse, paid for my vocational education at great personal and financial sacrifice. But this education served me well until my late twenties, when the chemicals in hairdressing became toxic irritants and the health problems that followed made it necessary for me to find work in business settings. In my early thirties, after a divorce, I entered the corporate world. Through the sudden poverty of divorce and even the financial struggle that followed, remarriage, and the emotional energy and economic costs of raising three children (including one step-child), the dream of a college degree seemed distant indeed.

During my life, I became self-taught through pursuing various interests and readings in a wide variety of areas. Later I was introduced to research while performing volunteer law reform activities. I gained some college-level learning from owning a retail business, an advertising business, community service, childrearing, and caring for elderly parents and in-laws. My knowledge grew in the areas of political science, human resource management, life cycles (e.g., government relations through legislative lobbying, human growth and development, general psychology, gerontology), and business subjects (e.g., marketing, personnel placement, and the like).

But enough about me. Let's look at what you can do and what you need to know to do it!

HOW MANY ACCREDITED SHORT CUTS
DO YOU NEED?

Since the 1970s, there have been many educational options available for adults (partial and complete learning programs) but they were not well publicized. In the late 1980s, when I began speaking to groups about fast-track methods for earning a degree, some individuals seemed concerned that the conference table in front of them was covered with more than fifty resource books about ADs and ASCs. Many in the audience had looks of panic, while others seemed confused. Their minds were put at ease when I told them that the books were displayed to show them the many possibilities available to them to meet their degree goals. In all likelihood they would find a few ASCs that could make their dream of achieving a degree come true. I assured them that it would not take as much physical energy nor impose as much of a financial burden to complete a degree using these methods, as it would to complete a campus-based degree. By saving both time and in many cases money, the audience members (and you) would not need to use all of the methods outlined in these many resources. Further, I told them that if they read the suggested additional readings, sent for the Regents and Thomas Edison College catalogs covering general information and degree requirements, and read through the materials for eight to ten weeks, and still had questions—they could always call me. In over nine years I have not received one phone call, except for those telling me they were graduating from college and calling to thank me!

UNFAMILIAR CONCEPTS

As Kurt Lewin said: "If you want to truly understand something, try to change it." I hope you will be changing many concepts you have about college when you read this book. In so doing, you will develop a new understanding about college degrees as they relate to your needs.

When you first look at unfamiliar concepts, approaches, and methods offering educational options—many of which you might not have thought were possible—it can seem like a lot of work to co-ordinate all of this new information to achieve your desired results. My goal here, as it was when I covered the conference table with so much literature, is to reassure you that there are a great many "user friendly" educational options to assist you in reaching degree goals. Like me, you will probably need only a few ASCs. But rest assured, it is very possible to complete a degree without the high cost in *time* or *money*.

YEAR-ROUND COLLEGE

No college has unlimited funds or the time to provide a multifaceted curriculum of courses that students may want or need in order to de-sign and complete their degree on a year-round basis. Often campus-based degrees require courses that are only taught once during the school year, or possibly every eighteen months. Many of these courses are required for degree completion regardless of their lack of availability. As you explore the testing connection and ASCs, you will find an abundance of subjects available to you—year-round.

SOMEONE TO HOLD MY HAND

Since testing and ASCs are independent learning methods, there were occasions when I felt isolated and alone. During these times, I would think that perhaps a campus-based degree might have been a better choice (someone to hold my hand). Every time my mind would stray in this direction, thoughts of scheduled learning, related campus restrictions, and campus-related expenses would send me back to the comfort of my self-designed, self-paced degree path. For me, designing, initiating, and completing a degree in this nontraditional way was exhilarating and significantly enhanced my learning.

HIGH-TECH VERSUS PENCIL, PAPER, AND BOOKS

Since 1990, a year after I finished my bachelor's degree incorporating the usual pencil, paper, and books, *testing out* has gone high-tech and related programs have mushroomed! The testing systems of the 1990s have expanded their delivery to include computerized testing as well as audio and video study aides. However, the fees for this technology are considerably more. Of all the fast-track methods currently available, *testing out* with pencil, paper, and books remains the most *cost efficient*.

When I wholeheartedly began my degree path in 1986, the ASCs that I used had been in place for over twenty years. But in just eight years these programs have grown immensely due to the use of technology: now off-campus degree programs may well include computers, television, videos, fax machines, and conference calling. And the geographic range of the programs has literally exploded: for example, for years Kansas State University had an off-campus degree for the state of Kansas. Now, through Mind Extension University (cable television), its off-campus degree programs are nationwide. Rochester Institute of Technology is national, and Regents College which until 1994 granted only distance associate's and bachelor's degrees, now has a distance master's program.

Still, with so many adult educational options to consider, delivered in so many exciting and "user friendly" ways, the testing connection (ADs and ASCs) has gone from a smorgasbord in the seventies and eighties to a full-scale banquet in the nineties!

FEARS EVAPORATE

Once you realize you really can get a degree by credentializing the lifelong learning *you already have*, or attempt new learning with academic success, you can become more active in the pursuit of your degree. Your fears of not measuring up to current academic standards will evaporate (or at least diminish).

There are no set formulas for success, and, contrary to what most people believe, a degree has never been a panacea. It is my hope that any fears (general resistance) you have that might be standing in the way of achieving a degree will be dispelled once you have reviewed the information provided here. You must want a degree or you wouldn't be reading this book. It's your call.

IT JUST KEEPS GETTING BETTER

From 1986 to 1993, during my group and individual presentations, an ongoing concern would often be raised that an existing program just discovered might not be available when a student is ready. Perhaps you may think a degree is a good idea, but you need time to plan for it, and still may have to put it off for a year or two after learning about ADs and ASCs. Don't worry that these short cuts will not be available in the future. As past and recent academic history has shown, if anything the programs or testing systems will not only be there, they will probably be better and cover more areas than they do now.

As I write this book, looking to 1996 and the future, the programs continue to grow and get better. Educator Jerold Apps has stated in his book *Mastering the Teaching of Adults* that information "doubles every four to five years."[9] Now that technology is part of the accelerated degree system, I predict it will triple!

---

9. Melbourne, Fla.: Kreiger, Publishing Company, 1991.

IT GETS EASIER EVERY DAY

If you find the idea of *designing a degree* to be exhilarating and facilitating, then these degree options may be just what you need. However, if as you read about these short cuts you think they would be cumbersome and confusing, perhaps these options are not for you. Either way, it is your decision. As many respected academics have said, "After high school you are a *volunteer* in learning."

WORDS OF ENCOURAGEMENT

The information and concepts in this book will help you find the starting points you need to design and plan any degree, including an accelerated (even a traditional) undergraduate degree using ASCs. It is written from the point of view of an adult (me) who first became a college student and through degree completion became an adult education consultant. This perspective, and the fact that I experienced these systems firsthand, will help you realize your potential and help you reach your degree objectives and life goals.

In the 1990s, America's colleges encourage the adult learner to consider degree completion programs by attending their campuses or one of their outreach locations for approximately a year to a year and a half to wrap up unfulfilled college degree work. Others, like Regents College and Thomas Edison State College, have programs that make it possible for students to work totally off campus with no residency requirements.

While accredited methods like those in the testing connection have educational integrity in this country, there are small pockets of academic hesitancy and public disbelief that ADs and ASCs can be used, in whole or in part, to achieve a degree. It has not always been easy to find colleges that openly assist you in *designing a degree*. But it gets easier every day if you know what to shop for.

Still, not one college that I have reviewed will permit you to wander around at random in any degree program. What I found were colleges that would make it possible for you to fulfill your degree requirements in a combination of *flexible* ways that meet a student's academic needs and overcome most financial constraints. This freedom within higher education can be very exhilarating!

2

Look Forward, Not Back

"Failure is impossible."

Unknown

ACADEMIC SUCCESS AND FAILURE: A SECOND LOOK

Don't torture yourself. Learning can be fun. Because all too many people think of formal learning as torture, at the risk of being overly cautious and repetitious, we need to discuss your perception of your academic successes and failures. You need to make lists of these successes and failures. Successes would be learning experiences in which your expectations were met. Any failures could be learning experiences that did not meet your expectations or could be due in part to mismatched teaching styles[1] and learning prefer-

---

1. "Teaching styles" refers to how formal education is delivered, e.g., lectures, group discussion, readings, independent study, audio and video courses, computer courses.

ences,[2] and/or learning deficits. With this list in hand, identify and compare your reasons for the successes and failures in your life. Once you understand these reasons, you will make better choices in your future learning adventures.

Even if you were successful in your younger years, you might still be hesitant to attempt college because youth is no longer on your side, and you have many responsibilities to juggle. Or possibly you may feel uncomfortable in formal academic settings. As you read on and find out more about your learning preferences, your perceptions and expectations can be more nearly met. Relax. If you are ready academically and know your best educational options, then any concerns you might experience about failure can be overcome.

IS *INDEPENDENT STUDY* FOR YOU?

Many adult students choose to begin their college work with *independent study*, while others add it to their more traditional degree programs. The backbone of *testing out* and ASCs is the use of this learning method. It lends itself to a flexible schedule, and it lacks the restrictive structure of a traditional campus classroom and schedule. This means you can study on your own and complete your degree requirements at your own pace. If this seems overpowering, think about how you learn when you are on campus. There, too, you study and complete the bulk of your college work alone, on your own time, in between scheduled classes.

If the idea of *independent study* excites you, take the mini-quiz (see Appendix C). If the results tell you that this study method is possible for you, and you have identified your learning preferences, you are, as they said of certain people when I left high school, "col-

---

2. "Learning preferences" refers to how and where (the conditions in which) a person enjoys learning.

lege material." If not, this assessment and evaluation process and these exercises will help you see if you need to sharpen your study skills to prepare yourself to be "college material."

As you assess and evaluate your academic readiness and past experiences, take time to step back and reflect on your most successful learning experiences. You don't have to do any formal, deep study. Just make a list of the most uplifting learning you have completed up to this time in your life. For example, one client told me she really didn't like the training her company required her to take to maintain her job certification. It was too dry, too boring, required too much memorization, and she didn't like the building where they had to go to take the course.

To find out your learning preferences and the best atmospherics for you when you study, ask yourself the following questions:

Do I study better in bright or dim light?

Do I prefer complete quiet or background noise?

Do I learn and retain more in the morning or late at night?

Do I prefer a desk and chair or the floor and a pillow?

Now that you have thought about the places and ways you prefer to study and learn, think about the type of delivery systems you prefer. To determine this ask yourself these questions:

Do I prefer the teacher and lecture method?

Do I prefer the teacher and discussion method?

Do I prefer no teacher?

Do I prefer audio/video tapes, books, television, computer-generated learning, or a combination of some or all of these?

Answer these questions for yourself, as honestly as you can. Knowing how you like to learn and in what circumstances will help you and any professional advisor or college counselor assist you in your search for the fastest degree path.

In addition to these assessment and evaluation exercises, *New Horizons: The Education and Career Planning Guide for Adults,* by Haponski and McCabe,[3] offers excellent suggestions on how to focus your learning. For example, they offer ways to improve your learning skills (to stop those cold sweats).

"Improving Your Skills"

How important are: organization of time? study habits? reading? writing? speaking? listening? mathematics? computer basics? use of the library? note taking? taking exams? Can I improve?

In addition, this valuable book has information on "Effective Study Techniques" (pages 139–66), which includes the following excerpt on textbooks, the mainstay of any college degree regardless of the methods you use to complete it:

A high-quality textbook is like a road map. It leads the reader who knows how to use it to a destination. It is natural that textbook writers think in terms of structure, and you can use this thinking to your advantage.

Haponski and McCabe go on to outline basic study skills, which in turn can improve your learning outcomes (page 140). The same holds true for testing systems. For example, if a study guide for a course or college-level test in political science lists as its basic content 30 percent on United States government and 10 percent on international conflicts, then obviously it's a waste of time reading a

---

3. Princeton, N.J.: Peterson's Guides, 1992.

thousand-page book on international conflict and a brief volume on United States government. This holds true in studying a subject no matter what ASCs you decide to use.

A PLACE TO CALL YOUR OWN

In addition, Haponski and McCabe suggest (pages 173–74) that all students make a home study area. A study area is essential regardless of the level of study or the degree program. You need to set aside an area of your home that can accommodate books, papers, computers, and a desk that should lend itself to your personal study needs. This is a place you can call your own, where you can leave your study materials undisturbed when you are not there. It is important for a busy adult to be able to drop study projects and pick them up again without wasting valuable time in setup and tear-down. And you need to have a place that meets your personal comfort needs and will accommodate your learning preferences, e.g., lighting, seating, quiet or some noise (radio, CD player, etc.).

A TIMELINE AND STUDY BUDGET ARE MUSTS

Once you identify your optimum learning and study methods and your degree program, you need to complete a timeline and a study budget, just as you do with household or business planning. Your timeline should cover the start and targeted finish of your degree (in years). Be realistic when you do this timeline. Plan for your degree on the long side of what you expect your degree completion to be, especially if your have a family and work full-time.

Administrators at degree programs that promote the "one year to a college degree" have told me that they try to be realistic when recruiting students. Still, a small percentage of students experience

life's "roadblocks," e.g., serious family illness, overtime, job trans-
fers, job changes, financial setbacks. In accelerated degree programs,
it can usually be arranged for you to drop out and rejoin the next
group of students when that group is beginning the same module you
were in when you had to drop out.

A Timeline You Can Use

The timeline you establish should be one you can live with, and have
realistic details that pertain to your life and goals. It can have as
many items as you need and can include those listed below among
others!

- Work schedule
- Family time
- Personal projects
- Relaxation periods (no school)
- Family vacation
- College-generated study schedules
- Private study time

- Test dates if *testing out*
- Correspondence course deadlines if part of your degree plan
- Semester dates, enrollment deadlines (if taking campus classes)
- Study plans/learning agreement deadlines (if applicable)
- Seminar and workshop dates (when they apply)
- Major life events that will occur over the period of time it takes you to complete a degree, e.g, weddings, high school graduation of your children, a child starts kindergarten, college

A Study Budget: A Month at a Glance

A study budget is based on a monthly calendar. Some students prepare their budgets for three to six months at a time. The elements of the study budget are similar but more detailed than a timeline and should include the following:

- Weekly work schedule
- Weekly and daily study time
- Class time (if necessary)
- Library book returns
- Daily family time
- Special bimonthly time with family

New learning can be almost hypnotizing. This monthly and weekly schedule has to be consistent, yet flexible enough to keep you on target (especially when there is a testing deadline) and still give you room to maneuver through the rest of your life. No matter what your age, sacrifices have to be made if you are going to complete a degree. The study budget helps you keep in touch with your family and work. It can prevent you from driving yourself to the point of exhaustion while you stay the course.

Before we move on, I would like to digress a bit to show you where I went wrong. Maybe my difficult and valuable lesson will help you see the value of a timeline and a study budget.

When I began, I started on a run and continued at a maddening pace for the better part of three years—a great way to burn out, and very stressful on my entire family. My husband and daughter had agreed to do household chores for me, just as they would if I had had classes.

While *testing out* and taking correspondence courses using *independent study* I ran an advertising consulting business, followed by Education Options. Since I worked for myself, I did have more flexibility than those of you who work on a fixed schedule.

Once I could see the end of the tunnel and my bachelor's degree was close at hand, I became blinded to my family and outside activities. During the last three months of testing, I was working full-time for a nonprofit organization, my daughter was in the Miss Teen-USA Pageant, and my son was getting married a month after I graduated. Panic at not achieving the passing GRE test score needed to graduate was every bit as tense and distracting as the grade pressure that many traditional campus students experience.

During one of my panic attacks, my husband stood in our dinning room, looked heavenward and announced, "I cannot take this anymore! What is the rush to get a degree so fast? What happened to the old way of going to school part-time over five to ten years?"

I answered with some mumblings about my age and about how things in the workplace had changed so much, but his concerns were genuine.

We can laugh at it now, and we can say it reminds us of stories about the "runner's wall of pain." But we are not alone in these experiences and the feelings they generate.

Many colleagues and students have told me that intense study has changed their close relationships forever—usually for the better, but not always. It is my firm belief that a realistic timeline and a study budget will help you and your family avoid (as much as possible) similar frustrating experiences. However, there will be times, no matter how well you plan or discipline yourself, when you cannot be with your family; even *independent study* learning methods have deadlines, e.g., testing dates, the final exam in a correspondence course, or papers due for completion.

One colleague told me that he and his wife also budgeted time just for the two of them, and they budgeted family time. Another colleague told me that his family decided on a project to keep the lines of communication open and to remain close during his degree completion time. His family collected antique miniatures.

As a family we agreed on the project, one that would cover a minimum of two years, since I was working full-time and doing college work part-time. We began with the selection and hanging of small shelf holders for the miniatures. Then every two weeks the family planned trips to antique shops and garage sales. We made a point to include the children in the decision-making process of each acquisition. When the miniatures were home, we all decided where each miniature would be displayed.

The joy for us as a family was in the planning, the outings, where we would eat, developing some favorite places to go together to find miniatures. The children began reading library books on antique miniatures, and became knowledgeable in the world of miniature collectibles.

I can honestly say, as a family we grew closer together while I completed a degree. As it turned out, my overtime at work interrupted my college work, and it took me longer than we originally thought. But even if it had taken two short years, that's a long time to go your "separate" way from your family and expect to pick up the communication lines at the end of that time.

PLAN AND PREPARE

If you continue to consider ADs using ASCs that include *independent study*, do some serious thinking. If you find out you are a good candidate for this method of degree completion, keep in mind it is necessary to have academic proficiency in college-level English and writing, as well as reading and math.

Consider degree planning and preparation much like you would if you were preparing to begin a physical fitness exercise program. There would be certain prerequisites, e.g., a physical, followed by your choice of exercise. You would not get up from sitting in front of your television every evening and lift fifty-pound weights. You need to plan based on your goals, your schedule, and your resources. No one starts running without first walking.

Fully explore and think about the many methods available to you. Find out what you need to get *started* and to *finish*. Find the right combinations of degree elements and components, and develop the operational knowledge you will need to meet your goals. To help you do this, I have provided a checklist (see Appendix D) that will help you evaluate the various degree programs.

It's time to unlock your brain!

3

Unlock Your Brain

"Most of life's shadows are caused by our standing in our own sunshine."

Anonymous

BRAIN LOCK[1]

Do you still feel confused and unsure? Have you looked at college catalogs and brochures only to have your eyes blur and your mind go numb? Have you been so overwhelmed that you don't know quite what to do? If so, you have definitely experienced what I call *brain*

---

1. "Brain lock" is my term to describe how you feel when you have so much information that you are emotionally frozen, unable to do anything.

lock. If you answered yes to any of these questions, it's time to *unlock your brain and get started on your future*!

I, too, found my eyes glazing over and brain lock setting in after reading mounds of college literature, and it paralyzed me with inaction for over twenty years. Finally, I combined lifelong learning from my workplace with insights and valuable learning from a rich and rewarding life and applied them toward completing two accelerated degrees (ADs). And I did it with very little money, still making use of totally accredited methods.

How Bryce and Audra Got Started

Bryce's Story

Bryce called me one day in a panic. As the regional manager of an insurance company with direct supervisory responsibilities over fifty employees, it became clear to him that he had increasing numbers of employees who had degrees, but he did not. Bryce possessed extensive work experience, a few college courses from his past, and years of on-the-job learning that included insurance industry–sponsored training courses at seminars and workshops. I suggested he consider Thomas Edison State College, in Trenton, New Jersey, since this college can evaluate and assess all college-level work through the mail (he would not have to leave his job or his home). After making use of my suggestions (accredited short cuts), he called me eighteen months later to say that he was graduating from Thomas Edison State College with a bachelor's degree.

Audra's Story

On another occasion, Audra called, telling me that she was the president of a new bank and that she had made it through the ranks without even taking a college course. She feared that her employees would find out and her authority as their superior would be undermined. After learning about ADs and ASCs, she considered several off-campus colleges that would accept her bank training and grant credits for life experiences. Eventually, after testing in general studies (English, history) and a few other subjects, she enrolled at a college with a "one year to a college degree" program. Her total program took three years, longer than some, even though she did use accredited short cuts. But her goal was to obtain the degree without going on campus for all four years of study, or interrupting her work. And that is exactly what she did.

WHAT IT TAKES TO GET STARTED

Once I decided that there was no turning back, all it took for me to get started was to sit for one College Level Exam Program (CLEP) test in English Composition and to receive my first college grade— an A! Encouraged by that successful experience, I reviewed the CLEP sample test guidebook to consider taking other CLEP subject tests. During this review two colleges were listed that accepted college-level testing in partial completion of a degree or to achieve the whole undergraduate degree: Regents College in Albany, New York, and Thomas Edison State College in Trenton, New Jersey. I wrote to both. After reviewing their literature, I decided to enroll at Thomas Edison State College.

However, I was not prepared for the college process, at any college, and so my enrollment at Thomas Edison expired. A year later, as my testing progressed and I learned more about ADs, I chose Regents College. But I remained an *open* student until I was a year from completing my associate's degree. It is my hope that you will review college literature, evaluate your degree goals, target the college you want the first time, and complete your degree without delays.

WAIT TO ENROLL

If you find that testing and other ASCs are the college methods you want to use to complete your degree, remain an *open* student. By not formally enrolling at the college you select (especially off-campus colleges) you save on fees and related expenses, e.g., re-enrollment fees. Don't worry that by being an open student you will not know quite where you are or how much you have accomplished in relation to your degree goals. If you have a firm grasp of your degree requirements (and you should), when you take a test, enroll in a correspondence course, take vocational training, and/or any noncollegiate learning from a community or workplace source, all these systems send you a transcripted score report, report card with grade, and/or a certificate. When you do decide to go to a college, these serve as unofficial transcripts. To secure an official copy costs $4 to $10 for each, whereas annual re-enrollment fees at college can be as high as $500. By way of comparison, sending for official transcripts when you do officially enroll can cost approximately $100 to $150.[2] My official transcripts cost $90 for all my tests and correspondence courses.

Degree Requirements

Before you enroll at a school, before you pay any money, know the degree requirements for the degree you want (including residency requirements) at the college you plan to attend, even if the college allows you to test out. This means you need to know both the number of credits and subjects required before the degree can be conferred. Education is never wasted, but why risk the frustration of misdirected efforts? It's a luxury most adults cannot afford.

In addition to reviewing college catalogs, I urge you to read the suggested works in the "Books You Should Read" section of this book. Review the resources at your library on adult degree pro-

---

2. These costs are based on transcripts from several ASCs.

grams and learning methods, and locate and attend any free public information sessions on degree completion at local colleges. These public information sessions offer a wealth of college information.

While it's true that the sessions are given to recruit and enroll students in the college's degree completion program, they speak the "language of a college." As you focus and plan, you need to know the terms that will make you a more successful student.

To evaluate any degree program and how ASCs will work for you, information from as many sources as possible is vital. As you evaluate programs in relation to your needs, ask yourself these four questions.

What are the specific degree requirements?

How many credits make up the degree?

How many do I have, and how many credits do I need to acquire?

Can I use the accredited short cuts (ASCs) I want to use in this degree program?

To help you answer these questions, use the check list in Appendix D. Using a check list keeps the process organized and reduces the number of surprises along the way. No matter how carefully you plan your degree, part of the joy of completing a degree are the pleasant surprises (no need for unpleasant ones).

WHAT MAKES A DEGREE?

Before you consider any degree, you need to know the basic components of all degrees so that you can interpret "the language" of the degree requirements:

General subjects and core subject coursework

Major, minor, concentration, and elective subjects

Semester credit hours and quarter credit hours

Residency, no residency

Number of credits needed for an associate's and bachelor's degrees

General Subject and Core Subjects

General subjects are the basic courses all students are required to take, e.g., English, history, math, science, and the like. Core subjects are those required by each college (arts and sciences, engineering, and others), e.g., sociology, economics, general psychology, physical education, to name a few. Both general and core subjects can have enhanced names such as English Composition, Freshman English, English 101/102, College Algebra, Math for Liberal Arts, Western Civilization (history), Our Environment (biology).

Majors, Minors, Concentrations, and Electives

These subjects are as varied as the many colleges that exist worldwide. However, there are some basics that cover each of these subject areas.

Major subjects are the majority of subjects studied that name the degree (e.g., sociology, psychology, political science, history, etc.). A major usually requires thirty to forty semester credits for a bachelor's, and fifteen to twenty credits for an associate's degree; they provide the focus and specialty of academic study for the degree. For instance, a business major might include courses or coursework in organizational management, business policy, organizational communication, organizational structure and design, advanced strategic management, organizational behavior, decision making, small business management, introduction to business, etc.

Minors and concentrations are similar. They can require fifteen to twenty semester credits in a bachelor's degree and nine to twelve credits in an associate's degree in a subject area different from the major. For instance, a minor concentration for an economics major might be business subjects like international business, international finance, international management, international marketing, market research. Concentrations can also mean that you must earn credits in a certain number of broad subjects specifically required by the college in which you are enrolled. Each college has different but similar concentration requirements: e.g., nine to twelve semester credits in social sciences, general science, and general studies. Core curriculums are often called concentrations.

Electives are credits you take to satisfy the required number of credits needed for the degree but they are in areas fully chosen by you based on your interests. Most colleges require twelve to fifteen semester credits in a bachelor's degree, and six to twelve credits in an associate's degree. These credits do not have to be subjects directly related to the degree. In a business degree they could be labor relations, basic computer skills, business and contract law, consumer decision processes, writing for business and industry, industrial psychology—or horticulture, self-defense courses, radio and television production, analysis and interpretation of literature, parks and recreation, psychology of speech communication, or any other college-level subjects.

Semester credits and *quarter credits* refer to the number each course has in credits hours. The most popular academic increments are in 3 or 6 semester credits. Quarter credit hours are not as popular but do exist on some campuses, and in some testing and correspondence systems. Semester credits are based on the number of credit hours earned in courses lasting approximately sixteen weeks if taken on campus. Quarter credits are based on ten-week on-campus courses. Ohio University's College Credit by Examination is one system that uses quarter credits. Quarter credit hours (quarter credits) are the equivalent of 1.5 times semester credits. A 3 semester credit course translates into a 4.5 quarter credit course. And, in turn, the 4.5 quarter credit course is equivalent to a 3 semester credit course.

Residency is a term that refers to the number of required semester/quarter credits a student must take from a college in which he or she is enrolled for that college to grant a degree. Each college and each individual degree program determines the residency requirement. Going off campus does not mean that there is no residency requirement. Off-campus colleges can require a designated number of credits that must be acquired through the college's own degree programs and/or attendance at seminars and workshops the college sponsors or approves. To my knowledge, Regents College and Thomas Edison State College are the only two that have no residency requirement.[3] The number of degree credits it takes to attain an associate's degree is approximately 60 semester credits (90 quarter credits), and for a bachelor's degree approximately 120 semester credits (180 quarter credits). Colleges can vary on the credits they require, but for the most part this credit difference is usually targeted to require more credits not less. For example, a bachelor's degree at one college may be 124. An associate's degree may be 85 quarter credits.

A YEAR WASTED

When I was enrolled at Regents College and was working toward my degree requirements, the school's general subjects requirements

---

3. While Regents College in Albany, New York, and Thomas Edison State College in New Jersey do not have residency requirements, each has specific degree requirements for all of its degree completion programs.

read: Math/Science 3/3/6 credits. I interpreted this to mean that I needed three credits from each group. Wrong. It meant three of each for a total of six, or six of one (depending on the degree requirements).

In my case, after four years in high school of barely passing algebra, geometry, trigonometry, and calculus, and retaining very little of it, I opted to take a year of traditionally taught algebra at our local vocational college, at a cost of over $500. At the end of the year I took an CLEP algebra test, but did not achieve the required score to have this test accepted for my math credits.

Feeling as though my degree was slipping through my fingers, I called my student counselor (something I should have done a year earlier!). While lamenting at the lack of math for my degree, she told me that my degree would accept either all science credits or all math credits or both. From that point, I began studying for a CLEP General Biology test for six credits and met this degree requirement with three months of study and one test attempt.

COLLEGE-LEVEL LEARNING

The fact that you are reading this book demonstrates how motivated and dedicated you are to reaching your degree goals. At this point, in addition to taking the mini quiz (see Appendix C), you need to answer several important questions.

Are you a self-starter?

Do you like the idea of *designing a degree*?

Do you enjoy being responsible for managing your college learning?

Do you realize that all college credits require *college-level learning*, whether or not it is learned in a formal classroom at a college?

If you answered yes to these questions, and the results of the Mini-Quiz indicate that you prefer self-directed *independent study*, you are ready to begin.

VALIDATE YOURSELF

Now that you have taken stock and discovered you are made of the "right stuff," you need to take an inventory of your formal and informal learning, e.g., lifelong learning, vocational/professional business training. To do this you must begin to think of this learning in four ways.

Learning concepts and preferences

Philosophies of learning

Learning content

Practical applications of learning

Learning concepts and preferences are the processes you use to learn and store information. How do you like to learn? Do you prefer learning by reading, video presentations, or lectures? Do you prefer solitude, a class setting, *independent study,* or any combination of these methods? Do you need teacher guidance, or do you like being your own teacher?

Philosophies of learning can range from the very practical, job-based competency learning to taking courses because you enjoy the subject. Most adults I talk with want job-related degrees, either for advancement in a present career, or to help them make a career change. Your philosophy of learning will directly affect your choice of a college, and in turn where you complete a degree.

Learning content is the "nuts and bolts" of your degree. Just saying "I have lived life and have knowledge" is too vague. You must focus on the content of those learning experiences to translate them into their college-level equivalents. For example, you could say, "I learned estate planning when I handled my parents investments." Then you could ask, "What did I learn during this time that is academic in content, e.g., accounting, tax law, an understanding of the stock market and banking procedures? How does this fit into various college course descriptions?

What is the *practical application* of this learning? What do you want it to be? What do you need the outcome of your degree completion to be? Will it lead to economic advancement and professional standing, or will it be enrichment and personal satisfaction?

You Know More Than You Think You Know

Once you have honestly answered these questions, you can move on with your efforts toward a degree. If you're like most adults, you have lived life to the fullest, worked hard, raised a family, contributed to your community, enjoyed hobbies, read about numerous topics, and interacted with people. You probably possess some of what makes up the subject matter of a degree, whether you know it or not.

THREE EASY STEPS

Here are three easy steps you can take to familiarize yourself with what colleges provide in degree programs.

1. Get a phone book, a telephone, and ten postcards.

2. Look up the colleges in your area.

3. Call or write to each college and ask for its full catalog covering every degree program. If there are several catalogs focusing on groups of academic departments, request one of each.

When the catalogs arrive, "do your homework." Read through the course descriptions. Locate as many courses whose content most nearly matches your *life experiences* (lifelong learning) in all areas of your life, subjects you were good at in high school, and areas of study you will need in order to complete the degree you want. Remember, all degrees have concentrations and electives. This review of course descriptions will give you the grounding you need even if you select an off-campus degree or elect to test out.

Treat this search just as you would if you were choosing an investment for your retirement, because when you think about it—it is just that! As with an investment portfolio, keep track of this information. Make check lists of what is important to you for degree completion (see Appendix D).

As you assess various ADs, and the colleges that offer them (on/off campus), you will gain knowledge of which programs match your needs. Should you consider *testing out*, you will match these course descriptions to your lifelong leaning, or subjects you need for a degree, and connect this information with testing content descriptions.

Now that you are aware of ADs and ASCs, and have taken action to continue to develop your operational knowledge, you are ready to go shopping.

Your shopping trip begins!

4

Shop, Shop, Shop

"There are years that ask questions, and years that answer."

Zora Neale Hurston

A SHOPPING ADVENTURE AWAITS YOU

This chapter and the next will help you get down to the nitty-gritty of learning what options are available to you in seeking a degree. As one of my learned colleagues has said many times, "You are a consumer when it comes to education. You should demand your money's worth." How true! *I know of no other product or service that you first pay for and are then told by the seller or vendor what you will buy.*

A Mini Shopping List

You need to know your educational options if you expect to make an informed decision on your investment in a degree program. At this point, you have read college catalogs and brochures. Once you develop an operational knowledge of accredited short cuts (ASCs), you can match them with your formal and informal learning. With this information in hand, you can find the colleges you are interested in attending—on campus, off campus, or both—and how many ASCs they will accept for credit. Here is a mini shopping list.

Select your college

Secure degree requirements

Decide which accredited short cuts you can use

This primary list may be short, but it has many sublists. The third item has a sub-list that contains the following group of ASCs.

College-Level Exams:[1]

College Level Exam Program (CLEP)

American College Testing Proficiency Exam Program: Regents College Examinations (PEP:RCE)

Ohio University—Course Credit by Examination (CCE)

Defense Activity of Non-Traditional Support (DANTES)

---

1. Testing systems listed here and throughout this book can stand alone as college credits. They do not need to be implemented in conjunction with a degree unless the student is enrolled or enrolls in a degree program that accepts college-level testing for degree completion credits.

Departmental exams from local colleges

Technical and vocational exams

Challenge exams

Advance Placement Program (APP)

Foreign language proficiency exams

Video College Course Exams

College-level correspondence courses

Life credits using portfolio assessment

Co-op Education

Noncollegiate learning:

Business and industry training

Professional workshops and seminars

Banking and healthcare training and vocational education

Diploma education from vocational school, state funded schools, and proprietary schools

Military training and related coursework:

Formal military training, basic and ongoing

United States Armed Forces Institute (USAFI) courses

DANTES testing[2]

---

2. DANTES testing is listed twice. It is in the testing list since it is a test the general public can take. It is listed under military learning because it was originally developed for the military and many students who have a military background identify it as part of their learning.

College courses through the College of the Armed Forces, the University of Maryland, etc.

Miscellaneous:

Computer-generated degrees and courses

Reading, extension, television, video/audio, telenet courses and some noncredit courses

Trade school certificates

Licenses and certificates

Before we look more closely at each of these learning methods and systems, please note that each method of college learning will have different credits. For example, CLEP General Biology is recommended for 6 credits in the CLEP book on testing, yet a local college may allow only 4 credits because that is what the school grants in a degree program for its campus course. Similarly, Ohio University's CCE testing is computed in quarter credits, making its standard courses of 4.5 credits equivalent to a 3 semester credit course in the same subject area for a college on the semester system.

DOVETAIL DEGREE REQUIREMENTS AND CREDITS EARNED

This brings me to a very important part of your evaluation of ASCs. When you "go in and out" of several systems, e.g., a CLEP test, a correspondence course, a campus class, you need to make sure that the credits for each learning method meet your degree requirements. If not, you may think you have a certain amount of credits only to find out later on that you have less than you need.

Let's look at three college-level testing systems:

- CLEPs are exams offering 3 and 6 semester credits
- ACT PEP:RCE can be either 3, 6, 9, or 12 semester credits
- Ohio University's CCEs can be 4, 4.5, 5, or 6 quarter credits

If you need a 3-credit semester course, make sure a 4-credit quarter system course would be accepted. According to the semester/quarter credit formula: 3 semester credits x 1.5 = 4.5 quarter credits. A 4-credit quarter course would then be half a credit short of meeting the 3-credit semester requirement. However, if you are remaining an open student, you must make it a priority to match the semester/quarter credits to your degree requirements. If not, you may think you have the number of credits you need only to find out later that you have fewer than you need. *If fast is your objective, then this is important.*

TESTING OUT

Since *testing out* (with correspondence courses) was the main focus of my degree path, this discussion will take a detailed look at the "ins and outs" of the various forms of this degree completion methods. The remaining ASCs are discussed in chapter 5. The testing systems listed show you that testing is available in several standardized formats, providing several hundred subjects for college credits. Add to these the departmental exams available at most colleges, as well as challenge exams in specific courses, and it soon becomes apparent that the number of subjects available in testing to achieve college credits reaches into the thousands. However, you should focus on what you can do in your own locale through national and departmental tests.

As stated in previous chapters, the most well-known test systems are CLEP and PEP:RCE. Both systems are respected in the academic community, and are accepted sources of college credit, usually (but not always) without question.

Your "assignment" is to find out how many college credits from outside sources—including testing and the above-listed short cuts—are permitted in your degree program. Remember, all degrees, other than those from Regents College and Thomas Edison State College (which have no residency requirement), require a certain amount of credits (residency) be earned at the college that is granting your degree.

ONE OF MANY WAYS TO TEST

The following is an example of my course progression through several tests.

When I was studying for credit in Human Growth and Development, the child development chapter in the textbook gave the term "rooting" as the motion and action a baby makes when you touch its cheek. The baby turns toward your touch. Any parent or person who has held and touched a baby knows this action (experiential learning). The terminology was the missing piece I needed to complete college-level learning. Furthermore, I learned the names of the men and women who developed theories of human development. Prior to this, I knew many human growth and development stages, but by studying for the CLEP test in this subject, I learned who these leaders in the field were and their research findings, e.g., Pavlov, Piaget, Erickson, Maslow, Freud.

As I studied for Human Growth and Development, it was necessary to read books on general psychology. Since this meant I had formally learned a substantial amount of general psychology through reading and test preparation, I checked the content of that subject in the CLEP guidebook. From that content description, it appeared that with some additional study, I could take that test. Studying for the CLEP General Psychology test required some study in educational psychology. I later checked that test content, studied for it, and took the CLEP Educational Psychology test.

After those tests were completed and my scores were passing, I decided to look once more at my life experiences. This helped me focus on gerontology. My mother had been a registered nurse in geriatrics. When she needed family support in her seventies, she guided me through many phases of her eldercare. In addition, I worked on her estate planning, became her monthly business manager, assisted with healthcare assessment for her medical care, and oversaw various rehabilitation therapies when necessary.

PEP:RCE has a Foundations of Gerontology exam. After seeing the sample test, I began to study in the subject, tested for it, and received the required test score (grade). After that series of tests through CLEP and PEP:RCE, I felt I was on a "roll."

Another personal evaluation of my life reminded me that I had worked for a personnel agency and had accomplished other human resource management tasks at various jobs. The PEP:RCE Human Resources Management test (nine semester credits) sample revealed a content that seemed familiar to me. After studying for a few months, I passed that test. With all of these interrelated subjects, I accomplished a major in my associate's degree and concentrations in my bachelor's degree.

COLLEGE-LEVEL CORRESPONDENCE COURSES

While I was testing, some of my course work needed formal (guided) study. In Peterson's Guides *Independent Study Catalog*, a catalog that lists the National University and College Education Association's (NUCEA) top seventy-two rated colleges that provide correspondence courses,[3] I found several colleges with correspondence courses that interested me. The two colleges I selected were the University of Nebraska for advanced broadcast writing, and the Pennsylvania University for securities markets.

The cost of these independent study courses was approximately $200 to $300 each. I was provided the instructor guidance I wanted for these two subjects. The lessons were detailed but the instructions were easy to follow and the allotted time for the courses was more than adequate for me to complete them.

Most correspondence courses allow nine months to a year for completion, but can be finished in as few as six to eight weeks. All have provisions for extensions for a modest fee of between $30 and $60.

All materials to complete the correspondence courses were included. The following is typically provided in most correspondence courses:

- A textbook

- A course syllabus (outlining course objectives, assignments, etc.)

- Mail-in lesson cover sheets and envelopes

- Midterm/final exam requests, and related instructions

In 1991, two years after I graduated with a bachelor's degree, as I read through the various correspondence course catalogs for my daughter, I found a creative writing course through the University of Iowa Correspondence School. It boasted that its students' lessons

---

3. The NUCEA conducts educational marketing studies that have found that a growing number of mature students are using various combinations of *independent study,* including accredited college-level correspondence courses, in completing degrees.

were critiqued by workshop students of its world-famous graduate writers.

This reinforced my continued amazement and appreciation of the academic substance and creative learning opportunities of off-campus coursework. It has always seemed to me, and continues to be my impression, that colleges that provide off-campus coursework, "try harder" to facilitate the student's optimum learning, and pay close attention to the academic integrity of their course and degree offerings.

Incompletes Are Rare

Correspondence courses are difficult *not* to finish. You're always given enough time. And they have the same drop/add feature as traditional campus classes. Although I have completed three such courses, I have two incompletes (more about that later). As I mentioned earlier, during the completion of my associate's and bachelor's degrees I took Broadcast Writing from the University of Nebraska, and Securities Markets from the Pennsylvania State University. Both courses were very challenging and enjoyable learning experiences. After graduating with a bachelor of science, I completed a Writing for Business and Industry course from Iowa State University; it was NUCEA-rated in Peterson's Guide as both graduate and upper level. I also took Psychology of Speech Communication from another NUCEA correspondence college.

My Incompletes

During my undergraduate degrees, I had signed up for Parks and Recreation from an NUCEA correspondence college. This subject had been an interest of mine for years. It was a course I thought would be enjoyable, and would apply to my electives and enrich my outdoor spirit. When I sent in my first assignment, it received a low grade for "incomplete sentences" as answers to questions. The professor's comments were terse, in my opinion, since I had a warm and fuzzy experience through the University of Nebraska and a supportive experience through Pennsylvania State University. This reaction shocked me. Since I was on a tight testing schedule, I stopped working on the course. To me, complete sentences were not necessary in a lesson for parks and recreation, especially when one or two words were sufficient to answer the question. The professor disagreed. We had a falling out in the mail!

My decision at the time made sense to me because my testing schedule did not permit this drag on my time. I stopped working on the course and received an incomplete. Had I been wiser, I would have processed a "drop" for the course and sought a refund. Back in the late 1980s, when I enrolled in this course, I did not read the add/drop information on correspondence courses. Yes, my degree path has had many "no-nos" (guilty!) that this book is trying to help you avoid.

After receiving my undergraduate degree, the second course I took was Psychology of Speech Communication. I finished all assignments and the midterm. But taking the final exam to meet the course deadline was about to occur in the middle of a hectic schedule that included my entrance to graduate school for my doctorate. I petitioned the college to convert the course to an audit rather than take an incomplete, since my grade point average was 3.50. After two attempts through channels, both requests were denied, and I gave up. But I did read the textbook, the syllabus, and completed all the learning; I feel I have that course knowledge. Were I to need this learning translated into college credit, I would look for a national or departmental test in this subject.

As you can see, my use of these accredited systems caused me an impasse or two, but for the most part, accredited college-level correspondence courses facilitated my degree completion. It is my hope that knowing about my mistakes will help you avoid similar ones.

A TESTING SYSTEM SIMILAR TO COLLEGE-LEVEL CORRESPONDENCE COURSES

Before we leave accredited college-level correspondence learning, we need to discuss Ohio University Course Credit by Examination (CCE). This testing system is similar to a college-level correspondence course by having a specific book and time to study for the test (read more about CCEs in part 2). This means your testing is guided by a specific study curriculum. Other national testing systems have general guide materials, but this system provides guides that are content-specific.

COLLEGE CORRESPONDENCE DEGREES AND COURSES ARE NOT CORRESPONDENCE SCHOOLS

It is important to note that accredited NUCEA college correspondence degrees and courses are not to be confused with correspondence schools which report that their courses and programs are the same as, or actually are, an associate's degree. Some are considered associate's degrees, still their fees are high. Their "degrees" are nationally publicized on television, and their associate's in accounting is more expensive than an associate's degree in small business management with accounting emphasis from the Pennsylvania State University, Distance Degree Program. Frankly, even if the correspondence schools were less money and they do have valid, accredited associate's degrees, their "academic currency" is something I question compared to colleges like the Pennsylvania State University, a regionally accredited college degree in your area, or one of the many accredited distance degree programs.

GETTING THE MOST CREDITS
FOR YOUR TIME AND MONEY

When *testing out,* make sure you are getting the most credits for your time and money. This was certainly one of my priorities. I completed the requirement for both my junior and senior years by taking two Graduate Record Exams (GREs), one in Political Science and one in Sociology, for thirty credits each. These sixty credits put me well on the way to completing my bachelor's degree. For my associate's degree the most credits for the money was achieved by testing through PEP:RCE in Management in Human Resources for nine semester credits, CLEP General Biology for six semester credits, and two English tests: Freshman English for six semester credits (elective), and Analysis and Interpretation of Literature for six semester credits (elective). The four tests for my associate's degree gave me twenty-seven semester credits, nearly a full "year's worth" of credits. The two GREs for sixty semester credits gave me a full "two year's worth."

Now, lets look at the cost of these credits. Each GRE cost approximately $29 to $40: sixty semester credits for less than $100. The PEP:RCE test in Management in Human Resources (nine credits) was $125. Each six (semester) credit test was $29: eighteen credits cost me less than $90.[4]

LEARNING CAN BE FUN

As I said earlier, I found college-level learning to be a great deal of fun. But for some of you perhaps the thought of it is a bit frightening or reminds you of college experiences that you'd just as soon forget. Fortunately, as you now know, by the 1980s educators had dis-

---

4. These test costs are based on figures from 1986 to 1989. Test fees go up every eighteen months to two years.

covered that matching teaching and learning styles was the key to an optimum outcome for all education, including adult education. This philosophy has produced degree programs at many colleges that accommodate, encourage, and facilitate adults in their degree completion. This means that at last colleges, for whatever their reasons, have developed and provide some degree programs that are based on matching a student's specific academic and personal needs and learning preferences with college learning methods. In fact, most adult degree completion programs offer the choice of atmospherics and teaching styles to a growing number of mature students, e.g., special classrooms, traditional lecture hall, home study, computer center–generated courses, downtown business center programs near work.

At this point in your degree search, you need to locate colleges that have addressed these issues. Your ability to match teaching styles with your specific learning needs and preferences will increase your learning efficiency and help speed your college-level learning. Just imagine, learning that is stimulating and fun rather than dull, repetitious drudgery!

Keep shopping!

5

More Options

You Have Lots More Shopping to Do

"The person with the big
dreams is more powerful than
one with all the facts."

Unknown

In addition to *testing out* and correspondence courses, most adults
should consider the many other accredited short cuts (ASCs) available in degree completion programs that grant college credits for life
experiences, co-op education, and noncollegiate learning that includes business and industry training, military training, as well as licenses and certificates. Before you roll up your sleeves to concentrate on *testing out*, you should be aware of what these other ASCs
can do for you. This chapter reviews them to help you select the best
educational options for your degree path.

LIFE CREDITS

Life credits is a generic term referring to credits that can be granted based on experiential and noncollegiate learning. This learning can originate from business and professional training, noncredit adult education courses, and lifelong readings in your favorite subjects.

After high school most adults learn more than they realize. However, when it comes to college, adult students must match lifelong learning to college-level learning to receive credits in a degree completion program. No student can walk into a college and say, "I have lived twenty years since high school. Give me credits for living." *Life credits* granted to a student must have academic integrity, otherwise they would devalue the degree for which they are given.

PORTFOLIO ASSESSMENT

To receive *life credits* you need to know about portfolio assessment, a term introduced in chapter 1. It is a process that can be accomplished only inside a specific degree program, whether on or off campus. It is set up to demonstrate that your lifelong learning has merit as college-level learning.

If you decide to use portfolio assessments to credentialize your learning as part of your degree completion, you will be required to follow the rules and guidelines of this process. Each college uses its own methods and guidelines, but the assessment process has two very basic functions:

1. To identify and support the credibility of credit to be awarded

2. To provide educational value and aid the college and the student in determining credits to be awarded

There are some preliminary steps you can take, regardless of where you go to college, to make this determination of tangible college-level learning. Prior to any portfolio assessment, you should have sent for, received, and read college catalogs with course descriptions. Now you can:

1. Gather college catalogs containing course descriptions;

2. See if any of these course descriptions match or relate to your lifelong learning; and

3. Look at the testing systems listed in this book, send for their descriptions, and match them to your lifelong learning.

Once you are familiar with course and test descriptions found in these resources, you can concentrate on determining:

1. College-level lifelong learning that can be assessed for college credit through portfolio assessment; and

2. College-level lifelong learning that can be demonstrated by *testing out.*

COURSE DESCRIPTIONS GIVE YOU FOCUS

Reading college course descriptions will help you focus on the content and learning goals of various courses relative to your life experiences and the learning you have acquired from them. It will help you to describe your lifelong learning in terms that the academic community can understand and appreciate. Additionally, these terms will help academic advisors and assessment counselors assist you. Once you have these descriptions, it is easier to decide whether it is appropriate for you to use portfolio assessment to demonstrate your lifelong learning for possible credits.

As you work through this self-assessment process keep in mind my experiences. I used college testing to translate my work in business ownership and personnel for credits in management and human resources; what I learned while handling my parents' eldercare brought me credits in gerontology while my experience with their estate planning translated into credits in finance.

While portfolio assessment is popular with most accelerated degree programs, it takes time and involves paperwork. It's a process that takes patience and perseverance even under the best of conditions (i.e., a college that welcomes and facilitates it). This process requires faculty approval for each subject before you can receive credits in your degree program.

Even when guidelines are followed, I have seen the process waffle a time or two. No such problems exist when testing is used to document lifelong learning. When I tested in a subject and received the required score, that was the end of it. No paperwork. No faculty approval. I was finished with that subject, and the credit was earned.

In one of the degree completion programs I observed and worked with as a student counselor, the following portfolio assessments took place.

Louisa's Creative Writing for Credit

The student was a published writer. On the face of it, during student recruiting she was promised three credits in creative writing based on her published work. The actual work was college-level but the publication bordered on self-published and was based on the writer's ability to pay part of the publishing costs. The evaluating professor was furious and rejected the work. He refused to reconsider and/or offer the student any other way to demonstrate this learning other than taking a course simultaneously with the AD program.

My solution was to have the student take the CLEP: Analysis

and Interpretation in Literature (six credits) or a departmental test in creative writing from one of the local colleges. She opted for the CLEP test.

Jene's Life Experiences (Experiential Learning)

Jene had worked for four summers helping visiting missionaries with remote tribes. She learned to speak, read, and write the language the tribe spoke. On her final summer working with the missionaries and the tribe, she translated a chapter of the Bible into their language.

When she presented this for life credits, it was in two areas, foreign language and cross-cultural communications. She and I located academic course descriptions in a college catalog. For the language credits we presented both a course description, with a letter of verification from the missionaries, and a copy of the translated chapter to the language department. For cross-cultural communications we submitted a letter of verification and she wrote a summary paper of the four-year experience. She also submitted her journals for review. Jene was awarded the credits she wanted for this learning.

MY FAVORITE EXAMPLE

When I speak to groups my favorite example from my lifelong learning is in the area of horticulture.

When I was quite young, my mother would walk me around her gardens and point out the different varieties of plants. Though I was indifferent at the time, later in life my own gardening was very detailed and successful. If I wanted to complete credits for horticulture based on my experiential learning, I would locate an academic description of an introductory horticulture course in a college catalog. I would then find a testing system that had a test covering what I knew from a lifetime of horticultural work. Or, if I was in a degree completion program, I would take that information to the assessment counselor for portfolio assessment. In this way some degree requirements or electives can be met.

That's about me, but the following might jog your thinking about life experiences that you might use for credits. Planning and running a household budget and being in charge of the family banking might align with an introductory business management course and a basic course in introductory accounting.

Earn College Credit for What You Know, by Lois Lamdin, is an excellent resource guide on the general parameters of the portfolio assessment process (see pages 83–133).[1] One parameter she gives is to "avoid overkill." This process, as they say, does not require volumes of support materials: a verification letter from the organization where you completed the learning and a few samples of work are usually sufficient.

Another source that outlines portfolio assessment is *One Year to a College Degree,* by Lynette Long and Eileen Hershberger.[2] The authors provide excellent steps for completing a college degree in a year, provided you have substantial lifelong learning, prior college, and business training. They offer sample programs that will give you valuable direction (see pages 32–34). The book also covers an unusual portfolio assessment program called Assessment for Experiential Learning at the American University, Washington, D.C. (1980). Students earned credits for describing the knowledge they had attained from daily activities. Personally, I have heard about degree programs that have portfolio assessment included, but, to my knowledge this program is a rare offering in that it stands by itself.

---

1. Chicago, Ill.: CAEL, 1992.
2. Lafayette, La.: Huntington House, 1992.

If you're interested in a degree program with extensive portfolio assessment from a distance college, Empire State College (State University of New York), based in Saratoga Springs, has a worldwide distance degree program that accommodates "credentializing" life credits.

Check around. The available degree options expand every day, existing programs improve, and new programs are added. With a little digging you may even find this type of program in your own community.

As a final note on *life credits*, I have seen masters and doctorate programs that work with life experiences and allow them to be translated into graduate degree credits. However, for the most part, the portfolio assessment process is part of an undergraduate degree program.

Personal Choice: Not an Either/Or

Versatility is the key in portfolio assessment. Making the choice to use it is not necessarily an "either/or" situation. Some assessments combine several methods to verify learning, e.g., paperwork with oral testing, written challenge exams, national testing, and departmental exams.[3]

CO-OP EDUCATION AND NONCOLLEGIATE LEARNING

The next short cut you could consider is college-level learning from a workplace perspective. It is true that all ASCs can work for you, and your lifelong learning is interwoven, but I think it is important to look at collegiate and noncollegiate methods separately to get the big picture.

---

3. There may be a limit on the number of college-level testing credits allowed by a college in a specific degree program.

Co-op Education

As you read through college guidebooks written for adults, and traditional college catalogs, you will notice co-op education listed as an accredited short cut. It has national guidelines and rules, and is based on both employment and enrollment in a college degree program. Co-op education is available at over nine thousand colleges nationally at both the undergraduate and graduate levels. Each participating college has a co-op education office. To qualify you must be working at a job while enrolled at a college and taking a minimum of six to nine semester credits or equivalent quarter credits. If you are unemployed, in some cases (when possible) the co-op office, in conjunction with the specific academic department, will find you employment.

Your employment/learning must be connected to your academic program. Here's one example: you are a project coordinator, and your work is substantial in matrix management techniques and related total quality management. In co-op education there must be coordination between the co-op office, the business department at your college, and your employer. Once all three agree that your learning at work is relevant to your degree, and you meet minimum enrollment requirements, you can be eligible for three to six credits for one to two semesters.

As a final note, this is one of the few accelerated methods that can be used at the master's level. All others covered in this book are usually designed for and used at the associate's and bachelor's levels.

Noncollegiate Learning

Noncollegiate learning is separate from college-generated course work and is not dependent on whether you are enrolled in a degree program. When colleges refer to this learning they usually expect it to originate from business training, professional development organizations, and other noncredit adult education institutions such as lifelong learning centers at local colleges and adult education centers at high schools in your community.

Continuing Education Units (CEUs), which are both credit and noncredit and are generated from both lifelong learning and adult education centers, qualify for college credits if they meet degree requirements and academic criteria. CEUs are credits required by many professions to maintain licensure, e.g., nursing, teaching, radiation technology.

Evaluation of Noncollegiate Learning

To evaluate noncollegiate learning many colleges use the American Council on Education's *National Guide to Educational Credits for Training Programs*[4] as their guide. This annual publication makes evaluations of noncollegiate courses submitted to them for review and then publishes its recommendations to institutions in its Program for Noncollegiate Sponsored Instruction (PONSI). Colleges look to the American Council on Education (better known as ACE) for guidance when assessing a student's training. This guide lists nearly five thousand courses evaluated by PONSI. Even if your business or professional organization is not evaluated by PONSI, it may be similar in content to one that has received an evaluation. When I talk to groups or individuals who have extensive noncollegiate learning, I recommend that they review this guide. By seeing what is evaluated and the credit recommendations, you will be able to help any college assess what you have learned. Most library systems have a PONSI guide on their reference shelf.

---

4. Washington, D.C.: American Council on Education, 1992.

BUSINESS AND INDUSTRY TRAINING

While PONSI makes it possible to secure college credits for your training, not all programs qualify for this evaluation and endorsement. Nor do all programs provide the credits you may need. For this reason you need to recognize the connection between business and industry training and college testing systems. I suggest that you take a look at testing systems that reflect content similar to your training. When you see a match or a similarity, you can test in those subjects with or without studying the subject, depending on the depth of the learning you have acquired. This credentializes those programs in an academically accredited way.

MILITARY TRAINING

If you have military training and are a veteran, your *first stop should be the education office at the nearest military base*. These offices are usually up to date on national and local programs that will grant the most credits for your military training and experience. They are an excellent resource for one-on-one counseling concerning ADs and ASCs.

Years ago, when I was answering callers' questions on a radio show, a man phoned to complain that the local state college would grant only six credits for his Navy experience. I told him that this was probably all that the college was allowed to grant based on its academic policies. If he felt that this was the college he wanted his degree from ("academic currency"), he would have to accept its decision. Otherwise there were national and local colleges that could grant more credits, and he should check further.

ODD AND ENDS

The rest of the ASCs listed in chapter 4 cover computer-generated courses along with reading, extension, television, and telenet courses, and professional licenses and certificates. These courses can be taken independently in some cases and through colleges in others. You need to research these courses as you read college catalogs and guidebooks.[5]

Certificates earned in workshops, seminars, and professional training are a mix as well; they have to be looked at individually and in the context of your degree program and the depth of learning they produced. Professional licenses are accepted on an individual basis as well, depending upon the college and the license conferred. Some colleges will grant up to fifteen credits each for Federal Aviation Administration certifications, pilot licenses, and insurance underwriting. For detailed information you need to review the relevant section of Lamdin's *Earn College Credit for What You Know,* college catalogs, and/or check with the assessment counselor at the colleges you are evaluating for your degree completion.

SERIOUS THOUGHTS

Now that you know about ADs and ASCs, you can follow my discussion on *testing out* in the following chapters. Although this information is available to the public in libraries and at bookstores, there are no set or packaged answers. The completion of a degree path that is *right for you* is still very much *up to you.* Because ASCs can be individualized to meet your needs, *you* have to take charge.

---

5. While the accredited short cuts (ASCs) listed here are generally academically accepted, each college has its own list, which could contain more or fewer options than those offered in this book.

Many times students have told me that they felt like "throwing in the towel." Quitting seemed like the fastest form of relief from their academic struggles. Even with a simplified degree path and relatively low cost, discouragement can still set in. If you decide to use ADs and ASCs, you will be using *independent study* learning methods. You need to make sure you have a *strong support system of family, friends, and colleagues who can help you stay on track and minimize distractions.* In the "Books You Should Read" section of this book you will find suggested support methods and systems that could help you stay your course.

Remember, colleges know that a certain number of dropouts will occur even among the eighteen-to-twenty-four-year-old students, not to mention adults. When this happens, the college keeps the money you have paid. Very little of your tuition is returned unless you decide to drop a course in the first few weeks after your first campus classes or off-campus studies begin. And, if you are using student loans to obtain your degree, you owe the money whether you graduate or not.

This is why the low cost of *testing out* was so attractive to me. True, I was adding college credits to the education section of my resume, and I was credentializing my learning with academic subjects. But the cost was low, and I could pay "out of pocket," or quit any time, and not owe large amounts of money. This proved to me that the testing route was one of the best decisions I ever made.

COST COMPARISONS

As I said early on in this discussion, you must keep in mind that adult degrees are *big* business. One college promotion that grabbed me said, "2 + 2 = 12." This cryptic phrase means that a student can attend college by taking two six-semester-credit course modules two nights a week, yielding twelve credits a semester. True, students in the program need only attend class two nights per week but this arrangement called for two nine-week sessions covering the semester. The learning modules were set up to facilitate adult learning, requiring an adult to concentrate on modules rather than four or more subjects for an entire semester. Twelve credits per semester impressed me, until I found out that the cost per semester was $4,380 excluding books. That's a total of $8,760 per year for tuition. The cost per credit is $547. Furthermore, this was being offered at a small private college, not a nationally recognized college ("academic currency"). If you plan to pay over $8,000 per year, should you be going *just anywhere*?

Earlier we looked at the cost of testing per credit. Now let's look at the cost of credits on campus. A public two-year college offering an associate's degree charges approximately $50 to $75 per credit, making the cost of a three-credit course between $150 and $225. A public four-year college (associate's/bachelor's degree) charges approximately $75 to $150 a credit, making a three-credit course between $225 and $450. A private college (associate's/bachelor's degree) charges approximately $300 to $550 per credit, making the cost of a three-credit course between $900 to $1,650. These cost estimates do not include books, course materials, travel, or related expenses for class attendance.

Pieces of the Puzzle

I recollect one distance education coordinator telling me: "Finding out about and using college degree methods is like putting the pieces of a puzzle together."[6]

At this stage in our discussion, you should have a sense of the pieces of the puzzle that make up the components of an accelerated degree using accredited short cuts. You, like those who attend my

6. John Burke, Erie County Community College North, Buffalo, New York.

group presentations, will now need to take a chunk of time (about eight to ten weeks) to go to the library and read college guidebooks, send for college catalogs, and then read and digest them. Doing all of this helps you develop the operational knowledge you need to get started on your degree using *some* or *all* of these methods, especially *testing out*. Eight to ten weeks may seem like a long time, but it really isn't when you look at your ultimate goal of completing a degree. If you have not established your degree goals, and are searching for immediate starting points, this time for fact-finding will practically fly by.

Take the time you need to really know where you want to go and develop a plan to get there. If you rush out and sign up for something without looking at all your options, you really will do yourself a disservice. Prevent misdirected efforts whenever you can. You'll recall that I wasted a year and over $500 on a subject that I did not even need for a degree. Had I followed the above advice I would have saved both time and money.

Once you develop your focus and have created your "shopping list" by looking at various degree programs and methods (especially *testing out* and ASCs), you will know where you want to go with this information. You will know where and how to put the pieces of the puzzle together.

Be a smart consumer. Always shop around!

6

The Challenge and Rewards of *Testing Out*

"Too much of a good thing is
wonderful."

Mae West

TESTING OUT WITH REGENTS COLLEGE

In late 1986, I read a Regents College newsletter that featured an article about a man who had tested out for his degree in two years. By that time I had already accumulated a significant number of testing credits. Reading this, and knowing that total testing was a real possibility, added momentum to my testing quest.

At the time I read this information, I was still trying to decide between a local degree completion program and Regents College. There were three reasons for making Regents College my final choice for both of my undergraduate degrees: the cost was reasonable, the college was fully accredited, and it accepted college-level testing in subjects matching my degree requirements. It was possible for me to test in 50 of 60 credits required for an associate's degree, and 110 of 120 credits required for a bachelor's degree.

These two degrees cost me less than $3,000, including the cost of my roundtrip airfare from Wichita, Kansas, to Albany, New York, for my graduation. At 1995 dollars, these two degrees, including the airfare to graduation, would cost approximately $3,500 to $4,500.

THE TESTS AND SUBJECTS I USED TO COMPLETE MY ASSOCIATE'S AND BACHELOR'S DEGREES

Here are the tests used for my degrees in conjunction with campus course work, a workshop, and college correspondence courses:

CLEP

English Composition (with Essay)	6
Humanities	6
General Biology	6
Introduction to Sociology	3
Human Growth and Development	3
General Psychology	3
Educational Psychology	3
Introduction to Macroeconomics	3
Security Markets	3
Introduction to Marketing	3
Advanced Broadcast Writing	3
Your Future in Business (summer campus course)	3
Freshman English	6
Analysis and Interpretation of Literature	6

The Writers Workshop	1
ACT PEP:RCE	
Foundations of Gerontology	3
Management of Human Resources Level II	9
GRE	
Political Science	30
Sociology	30

Since I used the GREs at Regents College (my alma mater), the testing score requirements have changed. You can still use GREs for up to thirty semester credits; however, the test scores that Regents allows as of 1994 are graduated. For example, previously, as long as you achieved at least one score you were awarded all thirty GRE credits. Now, the minimum score established at Regents College provides you with three GRE credits. As your score rises, based on the college's requirements, the number of your earned credits goes up to the maximum number of thirty.

When I *tested out* for semester credits, subject by subject, each CLEP cost $29 for from three to six credits; it's now $50. Each GRE was $29 for thirty credits; it's now $64. The PEP:RCE test in foundations of gerontology cost me $40 for three credits; it's now $50. The test in management in human resources for nine credits cost me $125; it's now $140.

PRESSURE, PRESSURE, PRESSURE

While we are talking money and testing pressure, it is time to mention registering for CLEP and PEP:RCE. When you register for a CLEP, given on a monthly basis (except January and February), $8 of the $50 is a testing center fee. Should you decide that you are not quite ready to "sit" for the test, you can notify the center to reschedule you for the next month. When reregistering, the $8 has to be paid again, but the $42 testing fee is only charged once if you take the test. If you cancel and no test is taken, the $42 is returned to you. PEP:RCE allows you to reschedule as well. All but approximately $15 is refunded. This rescheduling is handled through the mail, and is more costly than CLEP's reregistration.

When you reschedule a test you give yourself a chance to continue studying. With CLEP the registration is handled at the testing center. This firsthand contact means you can even reschedule a test a third time, paying another $8. Things happen, and this rescheduling with modest reregistration costs makes testing workable with any adult's busy schedule.

TEST IN SUBJECTS YOU KNOW

When I first began testing for my initial eighteen credits, my test selections were subjects I was good at in high school, had read about over the years since high school, or had lifelong learning from private and public projects. One of the first CLEP tests I took was English Composition. Later I tested in Freshman English, since some colleges take one or the other. Again, had I already selected a college and secured my degree requirements, time and money would have been saved. Later, when I knew that Regents College was my choice, I needed the English Composition *with essay*, and eventually retook it to satisfy my degree requirement. Yet another waste of my time, effort, and money.

Let's return to my suggestion that your first testing attempts focus on subjects you were good at in high school or that are special to you in your adult life. Successful testing will encourage you, and spur you on. Testing in a subject that is new to you at the start might reinforce your perceived barriers and halt your progress toward your degree goal. There is plenty of time for taking chances after you've established a foothold.

After English Composition was completed, my next choices were in subjects that interested me from years of reading or in business subjects somewhat related to my workplace experiences. My successful testing continued with CLEPs in Introduction to Sociology, Introduction to Management, Introduction to Marketing, and Introduction to Business Law.

PEER CHALLENGE

English was always one of my best subjects. By the time I began testing I had been a freelance writer for over ten years. My score in the CLEP English Composition was a 591 of a possible 610. That was a heady experience. Not long after taking the test I was bragging about this accomplishment to a colleague. She challenged me to try a subject test, which she considered to be more difficult than the general tests like English Composition. She had taken the CLEP Introduction to Sociology test.

Her challenge stimulated me to register for that very CLEP test. This meant that I read a sociology textbook cover to cover for the next thirty days. I remember carrying that book with me everywhere. I took the test, passed it, and proceeded on to business subjects.

I *don't* recommend this spontaneous approach to test taking. While I was fortunate to get passing scores, and proved something to myself and my colleagues in the process, it was this "shoot from the hip" success that caused me to blunder into tests unprepared. I took several tests, which I passed, but did not achieve test scores that were high enough to be awarded credits toward degree completion from those efforts (i.e., Introduction to Business Law, Microeconomics, and Introduction to Management).

Testing Tip

At this point in our conversation, I want to share a testing tip with you. Those of you who do attempt an accelerated degree using ASCs in any subject should be sure to learn the major theories and the leaders in the field of research in that subject. This is a fundamental part of every college-level subject, including testing.

LEARNING AND TESTING PREFERENCES

When sitting for tests, I found it conducive to my success if I sat in the same place with the same person proctoring the test. I realized this after reviewing the low test scores I received in subjects that I definitely knew. Upon reflection I noticed that those tests were taken in a different test room, with a different proctor and in different lighting. In the room where I took most of my tests, I sat alone, but on these other occasions I was in a room with several other people and the proctor told us that no one was to leave until everyone was finished. In these two tests my tablemate finished early and began fidgeting. First she tapped the table with her pencil; then she took out her store coupons and began sorting them. Finally, I told her to put them away. With that the proctor told her to sit on the couch and wait for dismissal. I passed, but not with the score required for the three credits to count toward my degree.

Here's my point: be assertive and stand up for your rights. Sitting in a certain room and having a specific proctor were important to the outcome of my score, and ultimately to my degree completion.

TEXTBOOKS AND STUDY MATERIALS[1]

The only two books I bought during work on my associate's and bachelor's degrees were those in my correspondence courses. To ensure that I had the books I needed at no out-of-pocket expense, I learned how to work effectively with my public library system. Libraries claim they do not have textbooks. That is correct in the strict sense. They generally do not have textbooks that are used in most college classes. Even if the library did have a specific text, the book would likely be used for a full semester (three months). Basic library systems by themselves cannot provide a book for more than one or two months, counting renewals, on one library card.

Luckily, my family had three library cards. To secure the books needed to study for a test—based on the test guide—I would check them out at the main, downtown library. When the books were due, they were renewed at my branch library rotating the checkout process on one of my family's other cards. The books were rotated on each of the three cards until I did not need them.

This is an above-board method, since the books would be renewed, unless there was a recall of the book. However, in the three years of testing for my undergraduate degrees, no books were ever recalled. But you should be aware that there is a possibility of this if you select libraries as your source for textbooks. (Recall is more likely at a college library than at public libraries.)

The library was eight miles from my home. If you live more than twenty-five miles from a major library, distance might hamper your efforts in both access to materials and in renewing them. Although some college libraries use mail-in renewal forms for up to three renewals, these policies differ with each library system.

Using this method for securing text materials gave me, and can give you, the opportunity to have the latest books to study for tests.

---

1. As of 1995 PEP:RCE has textbooks available to match its tests, but this adds to the cost of testing.

As an example, when searching for the Samuelson's *Economics* (eleventh edition) designated by the CLEP micro/macro economics test guide, I was able to secure the twelfth edition at my library. This not only gave me the subject content required for the test, it gave me even more. After all, my objective was learning, not just *testing to get by.*

In the *1992 Official Handbook for the CLEP Examination,* developed by the College Board/Educational Testing Service, Samuelson's fourteenth edition *Economics* is one of the suggested readings. But even if the required text was not in my library, I would select a similar book. With the test content in hand from test guidebooks and test samples, I would compare it to the table of contents and index of the book. If it had the subject content and a copyright of *five* years or newer from the time I planned to test in that subject, I would use it. Supplemental readings could be older, but the main textbook you use for learning should always be *five* years old or newer.

When I do presentations, I give the example of the necessity for having the current recommended textbook. In economics, "supply-side economics" is a term that became "Reaganomics" during the 1980s. If you had a book in economics that was written prior to 1980, regardless of its economic content, it would not have this information.

Review and Workbooks

If you are testing in technical subjects, you may benefit from review and workbooks. This is an individual decision, since you know how many years you may have had in a technical subject, and how long it has been since you brushed up on that subject.

Sources for textbooks and review/workbooks, in addition to public library systems, are your local college bookstores. They can special order a book or provide you with a similar one. If it is a book used by campus classes at that college, you may have the option to sell it back to the bookstore. Review/workbooks usually need to be purchased new, although I have seen some very good editions in public libraries. Still, for your planning, if this is an important part of your learning strategy, it's best to buy them. The average cost for review and workbooks is $10 to $25.

YOU CAN BE YOUR OWN TEACHER AND TESTING COACH

We all know what a teacher does. But to succeed at testing you need to know what a testing coach does so you can combine these methods to be a self-directed guide through your degree completion using *independent study*.

There are "testing coaches" for high school juniors and seniors who take ACTs and SATs for college entrance and need the highest scores. These same coaches can be helpful to an adult who chooses testing. There are also test preparation courses for GREs as well as law and medical school entrance exams. If you feel you need outside assistance in test preparation, especially for the first few you take, help is available. Do not be shy about finding the support you need. To pass my GRE in political science it was necessary to consult both a testing coach and the Educational Testing Service on testing tips.

As your own teacher you can be your own testing coach. You'll receive a sense of satisfaction from selecting your study materials, finding the "keys" to each test you take, and then passing the test! In addition, your confidence will build as you select the required textbooks and locate additional readings. The "additional" reading materials in my testing program were much like those a college instructor would assign. During three years of degree work, my family made paths through the piles of books I had stacked on the floor throughout the house for several months at a time.

LEARNING DEFICITS

Before we go any further, you might be saying to yourself, "Sure, she could do it, but what about me?" It's true, I have an above-average IQ, and I retain information well, but I also have dyslexia (a learning deficit in reading) as well as severe environmental allergies (making some classrooms off limits to me). I have been told by many educators that multiple-choice tests must have been difficult for me, and perhaps they were. But I was *driven* to complete a degree. Home-based study helped keep my allergies under control, and learning at my own pace helped me read and comprehend so that I could complete a degree on my terms.

It's *your* turn. Go for it!

7

Testing Out

An Untapped Resource for Adults

> "You can play with the big
> kids now."
>
> Unknown

YES YOU CAN!

As you have read throughout this book, yes, you can *test out* in today's college degree programs. This chapter will try to wrap up loose ends in your degree planning by showing you how to validate new or prior college-level learning. However, college-bound students of all ages, especially adults over thirty, can benefit from knowing about the nationally accepted testing systems designed to help "bridge the gap" in a degree program.

We discussed this earlier, but it bears repeating: the most widely known and frequently used testing systems featured in this book have been developed by the largest testing firms or respected colleges in the United States. Two of the most prominently known are the College Level Exam Program (CLEP) from the College Board of Educational Testing Service, (ETS), which provides high school students with the Scholastic Aptitude Test (SAT); and the American College Testing Proficiency Exam Program: Regents College Examinations (PEP:RCE), which provides the American College Test (ACT). The Defense Activity for Non-Traditional Education Support (DANTES) is provided by ETS, and Ohio University's Course Credit by Examination (CCE) is provided by the Ohio University system. Advanced Placement Program (APP) tests are from ETS, and Foreign Language Testing is provided by New York University.

According to John Bear's *Guide to Earning Non-Traditional College Degrees*:

> In 1836, the University of London "invented" the external degree. Degrees used to be based solely on examinations and a thesis (graduate degrees). London gave exams, but not the course work to prepare for one. In late 1987, optional correspondence and audiovisual materials, study courses, and informal tutoring assessment were made available. Several correspondence schools offer nondegree preparation for London's exams.[1]

It is interesting to note that the University of London makes these diverse methods available for *all* undergraduate and graduate degree levels, including a doctorate, while here in the United States we relegate testing for the most part to undergraduate degrees.

The most well-known and widely used testing system subject lists can be found in chapter 8. In addition, I have included some lesser-known tests that can assist you in documenting both your academic and vocational learning, thereby securing college credits.

---

1. Berkeley, Calif.: Ten Speed Press, 1990, p. 178.

Testing Systems that Help You Get College Credits

Here is a more expanded list of available testing systems:

CLEP – College Level Exam Program

DANTES – Defense Activity for Non-Traditional Education Support (CLEP for military now available to civilians)

PEP:RCE – American College Proficiency Exam Program: Regents College Examinations

CCE – Ohio University Tests: Course Credit by Examination

TECEP – Thomas Edison College Exam Program

Departmental exams at local colleges

Challenge exams for *life credits*

APP – Advanced Placement Program

GRE – Graduate Record Exam

New York University Proficiency Testing in Foreign Language

DLI – Defense Language Institute

FSI – Foreign Service Institute

NCC – National Computing Center

American Payroll Association

NCRA – National Court Reporters Association

PSI – Professional Secretaries International

CCI – Cardiovascular Credentialing International

ASE – National Institute for Automotive Service Excellence

College Video Corporation Credit by Examination
(provides video courses for CLEP, DANTES, and TECEP)*

HIGHLIGHTS OF THE TESTING SYSTEMS

CLEP

This is an internationally well-known testing system that provides lower-level exams on a monthly basis (except January and February). Each test is multiple choice (except those with essay for the second half), with two parts timed at forty-five minutes for a total of ninety minutes. You can take up to three tests per testing session, except those with essays (two per session).

DANTES

These tests provide both lower- and upper-level tests, especially those covering vocational areas such as carpentry, automotive repair, air conditioning, and real estate. At one time only military personnel could take DANTES tests. One of the biggest breakthroughs in testing has been the opening of DANTES to the "civilian" population. Many of the academic subject tests are aligned with some company-sponsored noncredit courses or training and can translate that learning into college credits.

My appreciation of these tests, now available to the general public, is reinforced by Ruth Hendricks at DANTES/ETS: "DANTES and CLEP go hand-in-hand, like ham and eggs. Together there are eighty tests. The bulk of those who take CLEP and DANTES are over the age of twenty-six."

---

*Read more about this testing system in chapter 8.

PEP:RCE

Both lower- and upper-level tests are provided, along with a few that are considered graduate level (depending on the college). This system has a good series of tests that equate with business subjects, and an excellent series for both associate's and bachelor's degrees in nursing.

CCE – Ohio University Credit Course by Examination

As mentioned earlier, CCE provides both lower- and upper-level tests. In addition to standard tests, the university allows special requests, including design of a CCE based on the availability of academic faculty and materials in the Ohio University system. This system includes tests in aviation and vocational areas.

Ohio University Tests: One Step Further

CCE testing programs are similar to correspondence study, since you first enroll and then they send you study guides with the prescribed textbook on which the test is based. Once enrolled, you have up to six months to study and take the test. Each student is allowed one extension: *either* three months for $25, *or* one month free. The average cost of textbooks is $30 to $40 per subject. If you locate your own copy of an equivalent text, you are not required to buy the book from the system. However, CCE is up front in letting you know that any deficiencies or erroneous information learned from a separate text are solely the student's responsibility.

GRE – Graduate Record Exam

GREs were developed to evaluate the knowledge a student possesses in a major, a minor, and a concentration of subjects, as an indicator of the student's preparedness for graduate school at the master's level. The graduate school has a required entrance score that students must receive (along with an undergraduate grade point average) to be accepted by a graduate school, in most cases regardless of where your degree was received. Many accelerated degree programs will accept GREs in place of four years worth of credits in your major field of study (Regents College). Other colleges might consider GREs for fifteen to thirty credits.

In my case, I paid $29 each for three tests ($87), and $40 for one standby, plus $12 for two study guides ($6 each), yielding sixty semester credits for $139. Even at today's rates, two tests for $128 (plus study materials) for fifteen to sixty semester credits is a real bargain!

If GREs are permitted in your degree program, and you think this is something you really want to attempt, send for samples in the subject you want to take. After you have reviewed the sample, it might be advisable to take one for practice. In addition to the free sample test, there are test guidebooks that cost between $9 to $12. These guides, along with the suggested readings and the percentage of the test subject that is outlined, are sufficient for you to test your preparedness.

Departmental Exams

Departmental exams provide both lower- and upper-level testing depending on whether the exam is developed and provided by a two- or four-year college or a graduate school (some nursing graduate schools also provide departmental exams). In my years of looking for a variety of testing systems for college students of all ages, the availability of national college-level testing systems and departmental exams have opened up enormous possibilities.

Departmental exams approved by the college you select can be from any college you decide to approach, as long as it is geographically expedient. It makes no sense to select a departmental exam from a college in Washington state if you live in New England. If, however, you travel for business or pleasure and the cost of going to a far away testing center is not a problem, the whole world of departmental exams is open to you!

Wichita State University (WSU), Wichita, Kansas, has one of the most comprehensive and cost-efficient departmental exam systems I have seen. I am sure there are other such testing programs around the country, but I have personal knowledge of this one. WSU's tests are already available, and are similar to the CLEP and PEP:RCE tests. The WSU Testing Center told me that students can request a departmental exam in any subject that can be generated from the department that teaches the subject. The cost is similar to that of a CLEP, and testing schedules are based on the testing center being open.[2]

When I taught at various two-year colleges, I inquired into their departmental testing systems. Most allowed departmental exams, but the cost was as much or more than a campus-based class at the college. Still, this eliminates classroom attendance, homework papers, travel to and from class, and miscellaneous expenses that accompany class attendance.

Challenge Exams

Challenge exams come in two forms: departmental exams and a test that is used in portfolio assessment to demonstrate proficiency in a subject learned from life experiences. Challenge exams can be oral or written and vary in content, length, and method based on the student and subject. You must work directly with the college to pin down the actual degree requirements that directly affect the content and details of a challenge exam in either the lower or the upper level. Some ready-made challenge exams are found in the CLEP, PEP:RCE, GRE, and departmental exam systems for nursing and computer science.

2. Richard Pratt, Wichita State University.

Advanced Placement Program

Students leaving high school can use Advanced Placement Program testing for subjects in which they have college-level knowledge acquired in high school. This means they can skip taking that subject as a freshman, receive three to six credits in the subject on their freshman transcript and begin at the sophomore level. If the subject is freshman level only, then that subject requirement is completed through the test. Some colleges let adults use these tests in foreign languages, math, science, or subjects required for a major, in which case the APP test can apply toward the freshman-level requirements in these areas of study.

Business and Industry Training and Testing

There is much written in the area of education about how colleges accept business and industry training, including the PONSI evaluation and the recommendation of noncollegiate learning programs. What you learn at work or through professional organizations could translate into college credits by testing in the same or related subject areas.

You may be one of many Americans who have received years of training at work and/or through their professional organizations. Some companies have watched their employees grow and develop from high school graduates to top management positions due to extensive training. This type of in-depth training makes it possible for these employees to use testing for college credits. Examples of tests that highly trained management personnel can consider taking include:

PEP:RCE

Business Policy

Operations Management

Human Resource Management

Organizational Behavior

CLEP

Introduction to Marketing

Introduction to Business Management

Introduction to Business Law

The banking and insurance industries have extensive training certification programs as well. Many banking and insurance employees can consider any of the accounting and finance tests available through several systems. In addition to receiving straight credit for actual courses, their industry training provides courses that have academic acceptance at colleges that work with adult degree completion programs. Examples of tests that highly trained banking and insurance personnel can consider taking include:

PEP:RCE

Accounting: Levels I, II, III

Cost Accounting

Finance: Levels I, II, III

Introductory Accounting

Intermediate Accounting

Advanced Accounting

CLEP

Introduction to Microeconomics

Introduction to Macroeconomics

DANTES

Money and Banking

Risk and Insurance

While past training has been discussed here in connection with testing, future training should also be thought about in terms of testing. If training or employer-sponsored education courses are available to you as an employee, you can attempt to match the content of these company-sponsored programs with existing college testing systems. This way you can be learning for the tests you want to take.

OUTDATED COURSES

Many adults have some college in their background, and you may be one of them. The problem that you may face when returning to complete a degree is that the college you choose may not accept your credits if they are more than five years old. This is not generally a problem with campus-free degrees because they usually accept all college credits that fulfill degree requirements with the designated score (grade), oftentimes even if the credit was earned twenty to thirty years ago. But most campus colleges have time limits on accepting credits, whether they are their own or transfer credits. In my experience this means they do not accept credits that were completed more than six to ten years earlier, even testing credits.

Should this be a problem for you, it is easily solved. If you learned the subject once, and passed, even with a low grade, you can do a brush-up review of your learning, and *test out* in the same or similar subject(s).

TESTING CENTERS AND SCHEDULES

All testing centers and testing schedules are listed in the guide materials of each testing system. For example, CLEP tests are given every month. PEP:RCE tests are given every other month. Testing centers are listed by state and/or country and by the colleges where they are located. Here's an example of what a testing center listing might look like.

CLEP

    Alaska
        University of Alaska at
            Fairbanks
            Galena
            Juneau
            Unalaska

    California
        Most California State University campuses

CLEP (outside the continental United States)

    Bermuda
        Bermuda College

    Canal Zone
        Panama Canal College

    Israel
        Bethlehem University

    U.S. Virgin Islands
        College of the Virgin Islands

Mexico
Universidad de las Americas, A.C.

Puerto Rico
All University of Puerto Rico campuses

PEP:RCE

California
California State University–Chico
Monterey Peninsula College–Monterey
University of San Diego

Hawaii
University of Hawaii
Hilo
Honolulu

PEP:RCE (outside United States)

Canada
Canadian School of Management, Toronto

France
American University of Paris

Germany
Schiller International University, Heidelberg

Switzerland
Business School Lausanne

Virgin Islands
College of the Virgin Islands, St. Thomas

Most testing systems listed in this book share many of the same testing centers. CLEP texts are given at more centers than the PEP:RCE test, although both are located at an ample number of far-reaching, comprehensive testing centers. However, the lesser-known tests can be taken in a variety of settings and are outlined in each testing system's guide materials. Regardless of the testing system you choose, you can arrange to take any test at a variety of educationally related settings, or any college testing center by special arrangement. In some cases there is an additional fee separate from the actual test fee, e.g., Ohio University's CCEs, departmental exams, challenge exams.

TEST PROCTORS

Testing centers usually have staff proctors for all national and departmental testing systems. For tests from systems like or including Ohio University's CCE, it varies. Some colleges include these systems in their proctoring services at no cost, while others charge a fee (the amount of which varies depending on the center).

Most testing centers can proctor tests from college correspondence courses. Usually there is a fee for these services. However, many college correspondence courses and Ohio University's CCEs will allow proctors outside a test center. These proctors can be from college personnel, local educators (K–12), corporate education personnel, library staff, and clergy (it varies depending on the system).

> The test proctor for my CLEP, PEP:RCE, and GREs was the same for every test I took, with the exception of having to alternate test centers used for GREs (and that fateful time, as you'll recall, the substitute proctor let my seatmate's behavior go astray). Because I did so well at testing, and was allowed to sit where I wanted, I called my test proctor my "lucky charm." He usually blushed when I told him that.

When I needed a proctor for my correspondence courses, I had a choice. The University of Nebraska allowed members of the clergy to proctor the midterm and final exams of their correspondence courses. Pennsylvania State University required the proctor for midterms and finals in their correspondence courses to be working educators if a test center was not used. The proctors were verified by proving they were listed on a school roster where they worked.

For the Pennsylvania State University course, I chose the principal or guidance counselor at my daughter's high school. The powers that be passed this request to the newest junior high assistant principal, who knew nothing about the midterm, consequently it was returned to the college. After a few phone calls to the new principal and Pennsylvania State University, the midterm test was re-sent. This was extra work for me, but from this experience I learned to be more assertive with the institution or agency that agrees to proctor an exam.

A lighter moment came when my minister agreed to proctor my midterm and final exams for the University of Nebraska. After I finished the midterm, I handed it to him with the mail-in envelope. He sealed the envelope and turned to me saying, "Here, mail this." As I drove to the post office, I was tempted to rush home, steam open the envelope, and check the answers. I mailed it.

COLLEGE ACCEPTANCE

Most colleges, even traditional campus colleges, will accept testing credits in their degree programs. Each college determines how many testing credits it will accept and the *test scores* it requires for those tests to be accepted. As stated earlier, this means you need to find out *all the degree requirements from the college where you want to complete your degree.* Finding the number of testing credits that are acceptable from that college can save you the frustration of such mis-directed efforts as:

- Wasting time and money by taking more test credit hours than the college will accept

- Testing in subjects that the college requires you to take through it

THE INTEGRITY OF A DEGREE

When students study for their degrees on or off campus, some colleges accept C- or D grades in a small number of courses, usually in electives. Colleges that accept testing credits do so with test scores (grades) recommended by the College Board/ETS, the American Council on Education (ACE), and their own institution's guidelines. These numerical scores are translated into the letter grades A through F or the numerical grades 4.00 through failing, unless the test is taken as a pass/fail.

Should you be concerned about the integrity of degrees composed entirely of credits from testing like those you can receive through Regents College, Thomas Edison State College, or a college that accepts a generous number of testing credits? It's been my understanding from reviewing academic policies that the credit standards are slightly higher for a degree accomplished through testing than a degree that allows for C- and D grades from a traditional degree program. A grade point average in a traditional degree program accommodates a student's C- and D grades. For testing scores to be accepted as credits, they must be the equivalent of a C+ or above or you won't receive credit for your degree. However, many colleges want B or above from testing credits, especially if the subject is part of the major or a concentration in a degree.

Clearly there is academic integrity to a degree accomplished entirely or almost entirely by *testing out*. Testing grades are a "fish or cut bait" proposition. The subject must be known at a specific level of proficiency to achieve the required test score to accomplish college credits in a degree program. There are no teacher preferences toward a student on grading, no grading on a curve, no grading based on papers turned in and classroom attendance. I think you get the picture.

EXTRA TIME—EUREKA!

No test is perfect. At the bachelor's level I was having difficulty with my final GRE, which, if memory serves, I took four times. When an exam is difficult, yet you're confidant you know the subject well, it could be your reading and response time to that particular test, or the way the test is constructed.

Through speaking with cooperative ETS representatives, I discovered that you can *ask for extra time on a test*. If a test seems extremely difficult, especially if it's in a subject you know quite well or have studied diligently, you can request extra time when you register for the test, as long as the college you are working with has no objections. This, in itself, is good news to anyone with a learning deficit (reading or math) and/or testing problems, e.g., test phobias.

TESTING STUDY GUIDES

All national tests as well as departmental and challenge exams have study guides and sample books, or test samples available at low or no cost. Each test guide lists the content of the exams and the sources of the content, e.g., textbooks and academic journal articles. Test information comes from guidebooks or single sample tests and covers a majority of the test information. I found that working with each test was the best study practice.

When I reviewed a sample test, after doing some brush-up studying, I gauged my ability to test in a subject on whether I could correctly answer 50 to 60 percent of the sample questions. If I answered less than 50 percent of the questions correctly and felt I knew less than I should about the subject, I would approach this as a new learning experience and allow a full three months to study the subject, just like a semester course. The difference being that there was no classroom schedule or assignments.

How to Study with a Test Guide

When I began looking at testing guides, CLEP had general subject guidebooks with sample tests for English, mathematics, humanities, natural sciences, social sciences and history. The remaining CLEP tests in business, social sciences, languages, and math were in a CLEP guidebook with a sample test in each subject. Both of these guidebooks were excellent starting points for me, and their content has continued to improve over the years.

I used the CLEP general subject guidebook to study for my humanities test. While both the CLEP general subject guidebook and the CLEP guidebook to the subject tests covered the humanities test, I chose the general subject guidebook because it had detailed study information. The answer section went beyond providing answers to give information about the answer, e.g., a Russian ballet master and the other works he had accomplished in his career.

Furthermore, when I used study guides, I would learn what each answer meant after a question, not just the correct answer. In a sociology question, if the correct answer was Maslow, and the incorrect answers were Freud, Pavlov, Erickson, and Piaget, I would learn about the works and major theories of the others as well.

No Penalties?

When testing is used there are no penalties or incompletes for not passing, unless you are enrolled at a college. Most colleges allow one testing attempt per subject. If their degree requirements are not satisfied with one attempt, most colleges will require the subject to be taken on campus, usually from the college that is granting the degree. If you are an open student, working on your own, a test can be retaken based on the rescheduling provisions of the testing system you are using.

If you fail an Ohio University CCE, you must wait six weeks before you can retake the test. After six weeks, if you have not retaken the test you can reapply for a full six months to study and re-test.[3] The cost is the same for both enrollments, with the exception of not having to purchase the textbook again.

LOWER- AND UPPER-LEVEL TESTING

CLEP provides lower-level exams that can count for up to sixty semester credits of an associate's degree, and the first sixty of a bachelor's degree. PEP:RCE has both lower- and upper-level tests. CLEP and PEP:RCE have exams that are three to six credits for lower-level subjects. However, PEP:RCE has business subject tests that can be three credits for lower-level and three to twelve credits for upper-level exams.

Recently, PEP:RCE announced a new series of upper-level tests in humanities, social sciences, and business. The six new tests are:

---

3. Should you feel you know the subject well enough to take the test, you do not have to wait the full six months.

American Dream Part I (3 credits)

International Conflicts in the 20th Century (3 credits)

New Role of Reason and Philosophy and Society
    in the 17th Century (3 credits)

Religions of the World (3 credits)

War in Vietnam (1945–75): A Global Perspective (3 credits)

History of Nazi Germany (3 credits)

These upper-level humanities and social science tests have videos produced by the Smithsonian Great Teachers Series as part of the study support. The videos are not necessary for learning the material or for test preparation. However, for those who like visual learning (learning styles/learning preferences), the videos are available at a reasonable rental cost. In upper-level business tests PEP:RCE now has labor relations (3 credits) and human resource management (3 credits), both of which are additions to their counterparts in lower-level tests.

THE COST

Costs vary by subject and the testing system that provides them.

- CLEP charges $50 for three to six lower-level credits.

- PEP:RCE charges $45 to $140 for three to twelve credits.

- Ohio University CCE charges $29 per quarter credit for four to six credits.

- Departmental exams can be as low as $40 for three credits or as high as $200 (approximately, depending on the college that provides them).

TEST SELECTION AND CONTENT

You can select tests the same way you choose a college course, by reading the test subject description. Each test description covers the content of the exam. Unlike the standard campus course description, these test "descriptions" provide in-depth percentages of the various material covered in the tests. This gives you the opportunity to assess whether you know enough to take the test, or if it requires new learning on your part. Regardless of whether a test is for new or prior learning, the description helps you decide if this is a test to meet your degree requirements by subject and level (e.g., undergraduate or graduate).

The content of tests in guidebooks and/or test samples shows the teams of scholars (the academic team of professors) who determined the subject matter and developed the test. As stated earlier, the guidebooks and sample tests list content descriptions similar to course descriptions in college catalogs. Testing centers are listed with the registration forms that are required for each test.

Test samples outline the percentages of subject content and the suggested textbooks for study guidance. The following describes the content of the CLEP Introduction to Management test. It was one of my choices. I have listed the basic information I read through to decide if it was a test I would take based on my degree requirements.

INTRODUCTION TO MANAGEMENT

Description of Test

The Introduction to Management examination covers the material that is usually taught in a one-term course in essentials of management and organization. The fact that such courses are offered by different types of institutions and in a number of fields other than business has been taken into account in preparation of this exam. The test requires a knowledge of human resources and operational and functional aspects of management, but primary emphasis is placed on functional aspects of management. The examination contains one hundred multiple-choice questions to be answered in two separately timed forty-five-minute sections.

Knowledge and Skills Required

Questions on the test require candidates to demonstrate one or more of the following abilities:

- Special factual knowledge of technical functions of management.

- Understanding of theory and significant underlying assumptions, concepts, and limitations of management data.

- Application of knowledge, general concepts, and principles of specific problems.

Test Content

Manpower

Operational aspects of management

Functional aspects of management

Miscellaneous perspectives in management and business systems.

Suggested Readings

Fundamentals of Management (8th ed.), James Donnely, Jr., Homewood, Ill.: Irwin, 1992.

Management (3rd ed.), R.W. Griffin, Boston: Houghton Mifflin, 1990.

Management (3rd ed.), Harold Koontz and Heinz Weihrich, New York: McGraw-Hill, 1988.

TESTERS: A LARGER GROUP THAN
YOU MIGHT THINK

As a combined total of the most prominently used testing systems, it is fair to say that among college students there have been over 10 million tests taken since 1970. As of 1994, there have been over 12 million people enrolled at the 10,000 colleges in the United States. Of these, approximately one in six is participating in alternative adult education, including degree completion. In 1994, of this approximately 250,000 took CLEPs and over 65,000 took PEP:RCEs. DANTES (CLEPs for the military, now available for civilians) had approximately 40,000 testers; of those, 12,000 were civilians. Ohio University's CCE tests continue to have annual enrollments of over 14,000.

Choosing this method of earning college credits will put you in a group whose numbers are increasing every year. Although there is no accurate way to tally departmental and challenge exams, in one year nearly 350,000 students take national college-level tests. As you can see, this is becoming a more common and desirable way to earn college credits. It is one that many hundreds of thousands of students use each year to help them complete their degrees.

Are you ready for the tests?

Part Two

The Nuts and Bolts
of *Testing Out*

"Do not think you are necessarily on the right track just because it is a well beaten path."

Unknown

8

Testing Systems

Your Gateway to a Degree

> "Strive for excellence, not perfection."
>
> Unknown

IT'S TIME FOR AN EYE OPENER

It's time to sit back in a comfortable chair, prop your feet up, and see what is available in both academic and vocational tests. You've done your homework on accelerated degrees and accredited short cuts. Now take a look at what testing subjects await you!

These test listings with credit and lower/upper-level recommendations are current for each testing system as of July 1995. Future tests and those taken in the past can be used toward college credit, but, as always, it is up to the college you want to attend or are attending to accept the test credits and to determine acceptance of the lower/upper-level status of the test. These credit recommendations have been gathered from several sources, two of which are the testing systems themselves and the American Council of Education (ACE). All testing systems list test scores and their grade equivalents with the testing reports that notify you of the outcome. Additionally, the time for each test can be different within each testing system and is often different from one system to another.

When you review these testing systems, remember that each test has its own numbers and codes, separate from college numbers and codes. For example, it is up to your college to designate how it will match CLEP's test for English Composition with essay to meet your degree requirements. If the test is accepted, it is generally used to fulfill credits for English 101/102. Other colleges might require a CLEP in Freshman English with essay, or College Composition with essay for this degree requirement.

ACT PEP:RCE (AMERICAN COLLEGE TESTING PROFICIENCY EXAM PROGRAM: REGENTS COLLEGE EXAMINATIONS)

PEP:RCE provide both lower- and upper-level tests, costing $60 to $140 for from three to twelve credits.

TEST SUBJECTS

Abnormal Psychology	3
Accounting: Level I	6
Accounting: Level II	9
Accounting: Level III, Area I	4
Accounting: Level III, Area II	4

Accounting: Level III, Area III   4

Advanced Accounting   3

Afro-American History   6

American History   6

Anatomy and Physiology   3

Applied Music   4

Auditing   3

Business Environment and Strategy   6

Business Policy   3

College Composition   3

Corporate Finance   3

Cost Accounting and Analysis   3

Criminal Investigation   3

Diagnosis and Remediation of Reading Problems   6

Earth Science   6

Educational Psychology   3

Federal Income Taxation   3

Finance: Level I   9

Finance: Level II   9

Finance: Level III   12

Foundations of Gerontology   3

NURSING: ASSOCIATE'S LEVEL

Nursing: Bachelor's Level

Adult Nursing	8
Health Support: Area I	4
Health Support: Area II	4
Health Restoration: Area I	4
Health Restoration: Area II	4
Material and Child Nursing, Baccalaureate Level	8
Psychiatric/Mental Health Nursing	4
Professional Strategies in Nursing	4

CLEP (COLLEGE LEVEL EXAM PROGRAM)*

CLEPs provide lower-level tests at a cost of $50 per test. Each test can be attempted as many times as your college will allow, but you must wait six months before retaking an exam.

General Examinations

English Composition	6
Humanities	6

---

*CLEP guidebooks have tests that are no longer in use, but are listed in *Guide to Educational Credit by Examination,* American Council of Education (1992). If you were a test taker prior to 1978, check the credit and score recommendations in the ACE book.

Mathematics   6

Natural Sciences   6

Social Science and History   6

Test Subjects

American Government   3

American History I: Early Colonization to 1987   3

American History II: 1865 to the present   3

American Literature   6

Analysis and Interpretation of Literature   6

Biology, General   6

Calculus with Elementary Functions   6

Chemistry, General   6

College Algebra   3

College Algebra/Trigonometry   3

College Composition   6

College French Levels 1/2   6–12

College German Levels 1/2   6–12

College Spanish Levels 1/2   6–12

General Psychology   3

Human Growth and Development   3

DANTES (DEFENSE ACTIVITY FOR NON-TRADITIONAL EDUCATION SUPPORT)

DANTES are exams in college subjects covering basic degree areas as well as business and vocational/technical training subjects. Many of the academic subjects are closely aligned with company-sponsored noncredit courses and training programs. Each test costs the military person or civilian $25. Civilian testing is subject to a testing center charge that varies according to each center, and can run as high as $50.

TEST SUBJECTS

Art of the Western World	3
Astronomy	3
Auditing I	3
Automotive Electrical/Electronics	3
Basic Automotive Service	3
Basic Marketing	3
Basic Technical Drafting	3
Beginning German I	3
Beginning German II	3
Beginning Italian I	3
Beginning Spanish I	3
Beginning Spanish II	3
Business Law II	3

Lifespan Developmental Psychology	3
Money and Banking	3
Organizational Behavior	3
Personnel and Human Resource Management	3
Physical Geology	3
Principles of Electronic Communications Systems	3
Principles of Finance	3
Principles of Financial Accounting	3
Principles of Physical Science I	3
Principles of Public Speaking	3
Principles of Real Estate	3
Principles of Refrigeration Technology	3
Principles of Statistics	3
Principles of Supervision	3
Risk and Insurance	3
Technical Writing	3
Television Theory and Circuitry	3
War and Peace in the Nuclear Age	3

GRE (GRADUATE RECORD EXAM)

GRE tests cover specific subjects. They are developed by a committee of examiners composed of professors who are actively engaged in teaching the subject and are on undergraduate and graduate faculties in different types of institutions and in different regions of the United States.

The cost for each multiple choice test is $64. GREs require a few months advance registration; however, the test system allows for standby (walk-in) registration. If you choose not to register in advance, but then find you have confidence in your knowledge closer to the test time even though it's too late to register, you can take a chance and be placed on standby. This status costs an additional $35 and is based on available space on a first-come-first-served basis. If you choose this route, it is advisable to call the testing center and tell them you plan to be a standby for your GRE subject test. If they have a limited number of tests in that subject, and know of other standbys for the same subject, they will advise you of this and caution you that you may not be able to test. ETS sends extra tests in each subject because it anticipates standbys. It is rare that you would be turned away as a standby unless the test is in computer science (large numbers of people take that test every session).

Alas, high-tech has arrived at the GREs. ETS provides GRE testing year-round for computers. This service is available three days a week, at locations around the United States. GRE provides IBM and Macintosh software for computer practice at $80 for each version.

GRE test scores are based on the number of correct answers minus the incorrect answers, and blanks (unanswered questions) do not count against you. This is one test where guessing can lower your score.

SUBJECT TESTS

(There are no college credit equivalents for these tests. Each college determines the credit to be awarded.)

Biochemistry, Cell and Molecular Biology

Biology

Chemistry/Science

Economics

Education

Geology

History

Literature in English

Mathematics, Computer

Political Science

Psychology

Revised Music

Sociology

OHIO UNIVERSITY TESTING:
CCE (COURSE CREDIT BY EXAMINATION)

All lower/upper-level tests cost $29 per quarter credit. A four–quarter credit test would cost $121 plus textbook fee. The following is a list of current CCE test offerings with approximate credits.*

ACCOUNTING

Financial Accounting	4
Managerial Accounting	4

AVIATION

(Students for these tests must have a current pilot's certificate to enroll in the following.)

Advanced Aeronautics for Commercial Pilot Ground Instruction	4
ATP Ground Instruction	4
Flight Engineer	4
Flight Instructor Ground Instruction	4
Instrument Ground Instruction and Air Traffic Control	4
Instrument Instructor Ground Instruction	3
Private Ground Instruction	4

*Information on Ohio University CCE has been taken from the Ohio University Lifelong Learning Program: Independent Study Bulletin 1993–94. Course descriptions contain content only; all prerequisites must be checked before the CCE course can be taken.

(CCE's performance examinations for the following flight courses must be arranged through the instructor at CCE's independent study office.* This office will process your enrollment and supply you with a course syllabus. Examinations can be taken only in Athens, Ohio.)

Commercial Flight Course, Part I	4
Commercial Flight Course, Part II	4
Commercial Flight Course, Part III	4
Commercial Flight Course, Part IV	4
Commercial Flight Course, Part IV (Multi-Engine Option)	6
Flight Instructor Course	3
Flight Instructor Operations: Multi-Engine	2
Instrument Instructor Flight Course	3
Private Pilot Flight Course	4

BIOLOGICAL SCIENCES

Bioethical Problems in Biology and Medicine	5
Biology and the Future of Man	5
Human Biology (for nonscience majors)	5
Human Physiology	4

*These exams have special instructions; the course content is given for general information.

BUSINESS ADMINISTRATION

Business and Its Environment	4

BUSINESS LAW

Law of Commercial Transactions	4
Law and Society	4
Law of the Management Process	4

ECONOMICS

301 Introduction to Economic Analysis	4
302 Introduction to Economic Analysis	4
304 Macroeconomics	4

ELECTRONIC TECHNOLOGY*

110 Basic Electronics	4
112 Solid State Devices and Industrial Electronics	4
120 Digital Electronics	5
134 Direct Current Circuit Analysis	5
135 Alternating Current Circuit Analysis	5
220 Electrical Motors, Control Circuits and Computers	4

---

*These courses are only for those who have life experience in electronics. These courses/exams are not to be used for new learning.

236A Microprocessor and Computer Basics   4

236B Microprocessor and Computer Basics   4

289 Electronics Trouble Shooting and Repair   4

ENGLISH

201 Critical Approaches to Fiction   4

203 Critical Approaches to Drama:
     Shakespeare, the Histories   4

302 Shakespeare, the Comedies   4

303 Shakespeare, the Tragedies   4

312 English Literature: 1500–1660   4

313 English Literature: 1660–1800   4

321 American Literature to the Civil War   4

341 American Literature   4

ENGLISH, HUMANITIES

107 Humanities: Great Books   4

108 Humanities: Great Books   4

307 Humanities: Great Books   4

308 Humanities: Great Books   4

FINANCE

325 Managerial Finance   4

FOREIGN LANGUAGES AND LITERATURES

French

111	Elementary French	4
112	Elementary French	4
113	Elementary French	4
211	Intermediate French	4
212	Intermediate French	4
213	Intermediate French	4
355	Introduction to French Literature	4
356	Introduction to French Literature	4

German

111	Elementary German	4
112	Elementary German	4
113	Elementary German	4
211	Intermediate German	4
212	Intermediate German	4
213	Intermediate German	4

Spanish

111	Elementary Spanish	4
112	Elementary Spanish	4
113	Elementary Spanish	4

211 Intermediate Spanish   4

212 Intermediate Spanish   4

213 Intermediate Spanish   4

GEOGRAPHY

101 Elements of Physical Geography   5

121 Human Geography   4

HEALTH AND SPORT SCIENCES

202 Health Science and Lifestyle Choices   4

227 First Aid   3

PHYSICAL EDUCATION AND SPORT SCIENCES

406 Organization and Administration
of Physical Education   4

HISTORY

Afro-American History I   4

History of the Black Worker   4

101 Western Civilization in Modern Times   4

102 Western Civilization in Modern Times   4

103 Western Civilization in Modern Times   4

211 American History to 1828   4

212 History of the United States, 1828–1900   4

213 History of the United States Since 1900   4

317A Ohio History to 1851   4

317B Ohio History Since 1851   4

329A Ancient Egypt and Mesopotamia   4

329B Ancient Greece   4

329C Ancient Rome   4

HUMAN RESOURCE MANAGEMENT

420 Human Resource Management   4

INTERPERSONAL COMMUNICATION

342 Communication and Persuasion   4

JOURNALISM

105 Introduction to Mass Communication   4

311 History of American Journalism   4

411 Newspaper and Communications Law   4

MARKETING

101 Consumer Survival in the Marketplace   4

301 Marketing Principles   4

MATHEMATICS

101 Basic Mathematics   4

113 Algebra   5

120 Elementary Topics in Mathematics	4
121 Elementary Topics in Mathematics	3
122 Elementary Topics in Mathematics	3
130 Plane Analytic Geometry	3
163A Introduction to Calculus	4
163B Introduction to Calculus	3
211 Elementary Linear Algebra	4
263A Analytic Geometry and Calculus	4
263B Analytic Geometry and Calculus	4
263C Analytic Geometry and Calculus	4
263D Analytic Geometry and Calculus	4
340 Differential Equations	4
410 Matrix Theory	4

MUSIC

Performance examinations (given only in Athens, Ohio) and number of credits to be awarded are available by special arrangement for courses in:

Applied Music

Music Education

Music Theory and Composition

Elementary education majors only:

160 Music Education: Music Fundamentals   3

OFFICE ADMINISTRATION TECHNOLOGY*

121	Introductory Typing	3
122	Intermediate Typing	3
123	Advanced Typing	3
131	Office Communications	3
231	Machine Computation	3
262	Report and Letter Writing	3

OPERATIONS

301	Principles of Operations	4

PHILOSOPHY

120	Principles of Reasoning	4
130	Introduction to Ethics	4
301	Introduction to Philosophy	3

PHYSICAL SCIENCE

100	Survey of Astronomy	4
101	Physical World	4
121	Physical World	3

---

*Examinations in some of these courses require qualified business education instructors to proctor them. Please check with the CCE office for further information before enrolling.

PHYSICS*

201	Introduction to Physics	4
202	Introduction to Physics	4
203	Introduction to Physics	4
251	General Physics	4
252	General Physics	4
253	General Physics	4

POLITICAL SCIENCE

304	State Politics	4

PSYCHOLOGY

101	General Psychology	5
121	Elementary Statistics for the Behavior Sciences	5
273	Child and Adolescent Psychology	4
275	Educational Psychology	4
310	Motivation	4
315	Behavior Genetics and Individual Differences	5
335	Environmental Psychology	5
337	Social Psychology of Justice	5
376	Psychological Disorders of Childhood	4

---

*These courses carry no laboratory credit unless one additional hour is earned in a regularly scheduled campus lab course.

QUANTITATIVE BUSINESS ANALYSIS

    201 Introduction to Business Statistics   4

SOCIOLOGY

    101 Introduction to Sociology   5

    220 Introduction to the Family   4

TECEP (THOMAS EDISON COLLEGE EXAM PROGRAM)

This testing system works in conjunction with all other national systems. Thomas Edison State College (TESC), developed the Thomas Edison College Exam Program (TECEP) for use in conjunction with DANTES. The cost of TECEP for TESC students is $50, and $100 for outside students (fees change yearly). TECEP tests are listed below, and DANTES are listed above (check with TESC for their DANTES list). These tests allow for two attempts, one repeat after three months if the required score is not obtained on the first attempt.

SUBJECT TESTS

    Advertising   3

    Advance Labor Relations and
    Collective Bargaining   3

    Alcohol Abuse: Fundamental Facts   3

    Anatomy and Physiology   6

    Art History and Appreciation I   3

    Art History and Appreciation II   3

Behavior Modification Techniques in Counseling 3

Business in Society   3

Business Policy   3

Channels of Distribution (Business)   3

Community Health   3

Counselor Training: Short Term Client Systems   3

Database Management   3

Financial Institutions and Markets   3

General Chemistry   6

General Physics I   3

General Physics II   3

Industrial Psychology   3

International Finance and Trade   3

Introduction to the Art of Theater   3

Introduction to Data Processing   3

Introduction to the History of Film   3

Introduction to Human Services   3

Introduction to Law Enforcement   3

Introduction to Operations Management   3

Introduction to Political Science   3

Introduction to Social Psychology   3

Word Processing Fundamentals	3
Written Expressions I	3
Written Expression II	3

CHALLENGE AND DEPARTMENTAL EXAMS

Both challenge and departmental exams are a mixed bag. Each college decides if it will offer departmental exams, and if so, how the exams will be developed and administered, along with the charge to be assessed for them.

Challenge exams are similar but are not generally "free standing" tests. They are usually developed as part of a portfolio assessment to demonstrate life experiences. For the most part they tend to be a combination of oral and/or essay examinations.

Departmental exams, on the other hand, are "free standing" tests similar to the CLEP, DANTES, PEP:RCE, and TECEP and can be considered for similar if not the same number of credits as the campus course in the same subject. For example, a campus class in minority studies for three semester credits could have a three-credit departmental test from that academic department through that college's testing center. Or the Minority Studies Department may agree to let you take the midterm/final in that course as a challenge exam. This would be a more involved route compared to the departmental exam.

COLLEGE COURSES BY VIDEO: CREDIT BY EXAMINATION

An emerging testing option is the college course by video with tests. Earlier we discussed the PEP:RCE series in which videos of the Great American Teaching Series from the Smithsonian Institute are optional. The tests for courses listed here are from Learningforce, Inc., but there are others available through local and national college programs.

These courses are very similar to Ohio University's CCE; you study the materials provided and then take a test. They differ in that each test incorporates the guided study of a video, along with a test based on the corresponding textbook. Learningforce, Inc. (College Course by Video) recommends the video as part of the study materials but it is not required. The program provides this service for Thomas Edison State College (TESC), CLEP, and DANTES. The cost for one of these college courses by video can range from $150 to $225 depending on the books and related materials, plus shipping and handling fees.

CLEP video courses (tests) are each worth three to six credits:

America: The Second Century*

The American Adventure

Business and the Law

Calculus

Calculus I

Communication through Literature*

Focus on Society*

Government by Consent

The Growing Years*

---

*No longer available, but can be submitted for credits by those who took it in the past.

Managerial Accounting

Marketing

Principles of Accounting

Psychology: The Study of Human Behavior

Writing for a Reason

DANTES video courses (tests) are each worth three to six credits:

The Business File

Faces of Culture

Marketing

Principles of Accounting

Project Universe

TESC video courses (tests)† are each worth three credits:

America: The Second Century*

The American Adventure

The Business File

Communicating Through Literature

Designing Home Interiors

---

*No longer available, but can be submitted for credits by those who took it in the past.

†These courses are available for enrolled TESC students.

Earth, Sea, and Sky

Faces of Culture

Government by Consent

The Growing Years*

Here's to Your Health*

Humanities Through the Arts

In Our Own Image

Interaction: Human Concerns in the Schools

Introduction to Biology

Introduction to Mathematics

Japan: The Changing Tradition

Japan: The Living Tradition

The Living Environment

Marketing

A Matter of Taste

The Photographic Vision: All About Photography

Project Universe: Astronomy

Psychology: The Study of Human Behavior

Quest for Peace*

*No longer available, but can be submitted for credits by those who took it in the past.

The Sociological Imagination

Writing for a Reason

USAFI (UNITED STATES ARMED FORCES INSTITUTE) STANDARDIZED SUBJECT EXAMINATIONS

As a rule, I am not listing outdated tests, but I feel that USAFI tests, given for the last time in 1974, need to be here for military personnel who want to use my suggestions in their degree completion. After 1974, DANTES and other testing systems were used in their place. However, if you have taken any of the USAFI tests listed below, many colleges still accept them for credit.

These tests from the armed forces have tested individuals in technical as well as academic areas. The technical tests are listed first, followed by academic tests. No credit equivalents are available.

TECHNICAL AND VOCATIONAL TESTS

SA 700 General Aeronautics

SA 710 Jet Aircraft Engine

SA 740 Auto Mechanics I

SA 741 Auto Mechanics II

SA 769 Introduction to Mechanical Drawing I

SA 770 Introduction to Mechanical Drawing II

SA 788 Introduction to Electronics I

SA 789 Introduction to Electronics II

SA 794 Introduction to Diesel Engines I

SA 795 Introduction to Diesel Engines II

SA 810 Technical Mechanics I

SA 811 Technical Mechanics II

SA 820 Technical Writing

SA 885 Fundamentals of Radio

SA 887 Intermediate Radio

SA 890 Radio Servicing

SA 891 Television Servicing

SA 893 Introduction to Television I

SA 894 Introduction to Television II

SA 936 Introduction to Refrigeration

SA 960 Introduction to Quality Control

ACADEMIC TESTS

SA 400 English Composition I

SA 401 English Composition II

SA 404 Survey of English Literature I

SA 405 Survey of English Literature II

SA 415 Speech I

SA 416 Speech II

SA 424 Intermediate College Algebra

SA 425 College Algebra

SB 425 College Algebra (Modern)

SA 430 Analytic Geometry

SA 433 Basic Statistics

SA 435 Plane Trigonometry

SA 440 Calculus I

SA 441 Calculus II

SA 442 Analytic Geometry and Calculus I

SA 443 Analytic Geometry and Calculus II

SA 444 Analytic Geometry and Calculus III

SA 445 Differential Equations

SA 446 Linear Algebra

SA 453 Principles of Economics I

SA 454 Principles of Economics II

SA 455 History of the United States I

SA 456 History of the United States II

SA 457 History of Civilization I

SA 458 History of Civilization II

SA 459 Modern European History I

SA 460 Modern European History II

SA 463 Russian History I

SA 464 Russian History II

SA 465 Latin American History I

SA 466 Latin American History II

SA 467 History of Modern East Asia

SA 468 History of Southeast Asia

SA 469 History of the Middle East

SA 472 Problems of Contemporary Latin America

SA 475 American Government I

SA 476 American Government II

SA 479 International Relations

SA 481 Modern European Governments

SA 482 Modern Asian Governments

SA 485 General Psychology

SA 488 Psychology of Personality and Adjustment

SA 495 Introductory Sociology

SA 496 Sociology II (Social Problems)

SA 498 Criminology

SB 498 Criminology

SA 500 Astronomy

SA 503 College Biology I

SA 504 College Biology II

SB 504 College Biology III

SA 507 Hygiene (Healthful Living)

SA 510 Oceanography

SA 512 Survey of Physical Science I

SA 513 Survey of Physical Science II

SA 514 College Chemistry I

SA 515 College Chemistry II

SA 517 College Physics I

SB 517 College Physics I

SA 518 College Physics II

SA 519 Geology I

SA 520 Geology II

SA 521 College Geography (Physical)

SA 522 College Geography (Cultural)

SA 523 Elements of Geography

SA 525 Principles of Accounting I

SA 526 Principles of Accounting II

SA 527 Intermediate Accounting

SA 533 Business Law I

SA 534 Business Law II

SA 535 Introduction to Data Processing

SA 539 Principles of Management

SA 543 Introduction to Business

SB 543 Introduction to Business

SA 544 Personnel Management

SA 545 Office Management

SA 546 Risk and Insurance

SA 547 Introduction to Real Estate

SA 549 Marketing

SA 575 Beginning Latin I

SA 575 Beginning Latin II

SA 577 Beginning French I

SA 578 Beginning French II

SA 579 Beginning German I

SA 580 Beginning German II

SA 581 Beginning Russian I

SA 582 Beginning Russian II

SA 583 Beginning Spanish I

SA 584 Beginning Spanish II

SA 585 Beginning Italian I

SA 586 Beginning Italian II

9

More Untapped Resources

"Every stone in the road,
Every pebble in your shoe,
Has led you to this place."

Jose Hilario Cedillos

VOCATIONAL TESTS COUNT

This is definitely an untapped resource for you. If you have taken
tests in payroll, professional secretarial, automotive service, medical
certification, court reporting, and foreign languages you might be
surprised to see how many of these tests are being evaluated for college credits. If you are considering a college degree and are in one
of these professions that provide such tests, they might be a future
resource you never thought could be tapped. Test credit recommendations listed in this chapter with each test or testing system are

based in part on the testing system's recommendations and from the American Council of Education.

NEW YORK UNIVERSITY PROFICIENCY TESTING IN FOREIGN LANGUAGE

This testing system provides native speakers with an assessment of their ability in their native language, and is now transcripted from New York University. This is a documentation that can be used to transfer credits. Each exam tests four basic areas: comprehension of the spoken language, use of the written language in free composition, translation from the native language into English, and translation from English into the native language.

The cost for the test is $150 for a 12-point test, and $75 for an additional 4 points, or $225 for 16 points. This testing system allows for on- or off-site testing. Off-site proctoring is open to anyone with a bachelor's degree who works for an official organization. A letter requesting the official proctor and enclosing the requisite fees with all forms filled out, once received by NYU's Foreign Language Department will yield by return mail the language test and its accompanying tapes. The credit allowance for each test is determined by the college you select for your degree. Here are the languages for which tests are currently available:

Albanian	Chinese (Mandarin)
Arabic	Czech
Armenian	Danish
Catalan	Dutch
Chinese (Cantonese)	Finnish

French	Norwegian
Gaelic (Irish)	Persian
German	Polish
Greek (classical)	Portuguese
Greek (modern)	Rumanian
Haitian Creole	Russian
Hebrew	Serbo-Croatian
Hindi	Spanish
Hungarian	Swedish
Icelandic	Tagalog
Italian	Thai
Japanese	Turkish
Korean	Ukrainian
Latin	Urdu
Malay	Yiddish

DLI (DEFENSE LANGUAGE INSTITUTE)

DLI tests are sponsored by the Foreign Language Center (formerly the Army Language School), which coordinates the foreign language proficiency for members of the armed services. The accepted credits vary widely, so they will not be included here.

The format for these tests consists of listening, reading, and speaking. They do not have a writing component. Each listening and reading test contains sixty-five multiple-choice items. The listening comprehension test is sixty-five minutes in length. The reading comprehension test is two hours and fifteen minutes in length. The speaking examination is forty-five minutes in length, consisting of four parts. Questions are asked by a native speaker in the language being tested. These tests include the following languages:

Arabic	Persian
Czech	Polish
Chinese (Mandarin)	Portuguese (European)
French	Rumanian
German	Russian
Hebrew	Spanish
Italian	Tagalog
Japanese	Turkish
Korean	Vietnamese

FSI (FOREIGN SERVICE INSTITUTE)

These exams are Oral Proficiency Language Assessment Examinations. The test format includes three tasks: conversing with a native speaker on a variety of social-personal topics chosen by the tester, interviewing a native speaker on a topic selected by the student, and briefing a native speaker on selected topics and responding to comments and questions. Credit recommendations in this system are based on the test score and can range between two and twelve credits.

Tests are available in this system on the following languages:

French

Spanish

NCC (NATIONAL COMPUTING CENTER)

These exams provide both lower- and upper-level credits depending on the college and the degree program. Credits can be approximately three for each of these subject areas.

Accounting

Basic Computing Principles

Business Organization

Computer Programming

Computer-Related Mathematics and Statistics

Human Communications

AMERICAN PAYROLL ASSOCIATION

The Certified Payroll Professional Examination is one exam with many credits. According to ACE recommendations, this test is for both lower- and upper-level credits, with the possibility of eleven credits in all; credits are defined in payroll taxes, payroll accounting, general business mathematics, personnel administration, and principles of accounting. The current cost of this test was not available at press time.

NCRA (NATIONAL COURT REPORTERS ASSOCIATION)

This exam system has cut-off dates for credit recommendations. If you took these tests before 1995, review the credit recommendations in the ACE guide.

Registered Professional Reporter

Legal Terminology and Procedures	6
Court Reporting Procedures	5
English Usage and Office Communication Skills	6
Dictation/Transcription	6

Certification of Merit Examination

Advanced Court Reporting	3
Judicial Procedures	6
Court Reporting Procedures	5
Office Communications Skills	4
Dictation/Transcription	6

PSI (PROFESSIONAL SECRETARY INTERNATIONAL EXAM)

This organization was formerly the National Secretaries Association. Its six-part test provides up to seventy-seven credits with the possibility of additional credits in shorthand, transcription, and typing. This testing system comes in several dated versions. You need to review the ACE guide or work with an assessment counselor to determine the subjects and the number of credits granted.

The following is a general overview of subjects that are possible from this testing system:

Accounting

Administration and Organization

Automated Office Administration

Business Communications

Business Law

Business Management

Human Relations in Business

Organizational Behavior

Principles of Human Resources

Management

Secretarial Skills
(shorthand, transcription, typing, and/or office procedures)

CCI (CARDIOVASCULAR CREDENTIALING INTERNATIONAL)

CCI provides three tests for health-care professionals, the cost of which is determined by each test.

Cardiovascular Registry Examination–Invasive   7

Cardiovascular Registry Examination–Noninvasive   12

Certified Cardiographic Technician Test   6

ASE (NATIONAL INSTITUTE FOR AUTOMOTIVE SERVICE EXCELLENCE)

The credits obtained are usually used in fulfilling technical degrees. Credit recommendations for these tests have been based on the vocational/technical degrees and lower-level subjects in an associate's or bachelor's degree that have accepted them in the past. In addition to meeting the ASE minimum score on the written tests, candidates who want ASE certification must also have appropriate hands-on experience in the speciality area. The college that accepts these tests will have guidelines to verify your hands-on experience.

AUTOMOBILE TESTS
(Credits can be one to three depending on the college.)

> Automotive Transmission/Transaxle
>
> Brakes
>
> Electrical Systems
>
> Engine Performance
>
> Engine Repair
>
> Heating and Air Conditioning
>
> Manual Drive Train and Axles
>
> Suspension and Steering

AUTO BODY TESTS
(Credit can be three to six depending on the college.)

> Body Repair
>
> Painting and Refinishing

HEAVY-DUTY TRUCK TESTS
(Credits can be three to six depending on the college.)

> Brakes
>
> Diesel Engines

Drive Train

Electrical Systems

Gasoline Engines

Suspension and Steering

GED (GENERAL EDUCATIONAL DEVELOPMENT)

GED tests have provided some students with college credits. All four tests can be considered, depending on the college you are working with to complete your degree. As an aside to the college credits, in my work I have met many accomplished, articulate adults without a high school diploma (a few are eighth grade graduates!). Even if a degree is not in your immediate thoughts, preparing and taking the GED might be to your advantage, If nothing else, it can help you prove to yourself that you can *test out*. And, while we're discussing high school graduation, some colleges will waive the requirement for a high school diploma based on your life experiences!

Appendix A

Test Comparison

In this section I compare the content of the four tests I took: three CLEP (Human Growth and Development, General Psychology, and Introduction to Educational Psychology) and one PEP:RCE (Foundations of Gerontology). These were mentioned earlier. It might help you to see how tests can be dovetailed, just as traditional campus courses work into each other. In each test synopsis the content will be listed as presented in the test guides, along with suggested readings to show how you can connect "courses" that interrelate through studying for each test. The recommended readings for these tests were taken from current CLEP and PEP:RCE study guides and testing samples.

Please note the copyrights on these readings are usually *five* years or newer. This reinforces my suggestion that newer books should be used for testing or for any *independent study* you plan to accomplish. Please note, the suggested readings given here are from the 1994 test samples but are similar to the ones that were suggested for the tests I took in the late eighties.

CLEP: HUMAN GROWTH AND DEVELOPMENT

RECOMMENDED READINGS

The Developing Child, Bee, 6th ed., 1992
Developmental Psychology: An Introduction, Gardner, 2nd ed., 1982
Developmental Psychology, Liebert, Wicks-Nelson, and Kail, 4th ed., 1986
Human Development, Papalia and Wendkos Olds, 5th ed., 1990

DESCRIPTION OF THE EXAMINATION

The subject examination in human growth and development (infancy, childhood, adolescence) covers material that is generally taught in one-semester introductory courses in child psychology, child development, or developmental psychology, with primary emphasis on infancy, early childhood, and middle childhood. An understanding of the major theories and research related to physical, cognitive, social, personality, and emotional development is required, as is the ability to apply this knowledge.

KNOWLEDGE AND SKILLS REQUIRED (90 MINUTES)

1. Knowledge of basic facts and terminology

2. Understanding of generally accepted concepts and principles

3. Understanding of theories and recurrent developmental issues

4. Application of knowledge to particular problems and situations

The examination questions are drawn from the thirteen major categories listed below. For each category, several key words and phrases identify topics with which candidates should be familiar:

Atypical development

Biological development

Cognitive development

Family and society

Intelligence

Language development

Learning

Perceptual and sensorimotor development

Personality and emotions

Research strategies and methodology

Schooling and intervention

Social development

Theories of development

CLEP: GENERAL PSYCHOLOGY

RECOMMENDED READINGS

Introduction to Psychology, Atkinson, 10th ed., 1990
Fundamentals of Psychology, Gerow, Brothen, and Newell, 1989
Psychology, Rathus, 4th ed., 1989
Psychology and Life, Zimbardo, 3rd ed., 1992

DESCRIPTION OF THE EXAMINATION

The introductory psychology examination covers material that is usually taught in a one-semester undergraduate course in introductory psychology. It stresses basic facts, concepts, and generally accepted principles. Among the topics included on the exam are learning and cognition, behavior, personality, abnormal behavior, perception, motivation and emotion, and developmental and social psychology.

KNOWLEDGE AND SKILLS REQUIRED (90 MINUTES)

1. Knowledge of terminology, principles, and theory

2. Comprehension, evaluation, and analysis of problem situations

3. Application of knowledge to new situations

The introductory psychology examination requires knowledge of the following areas of psychology:

Abnormal psychology

Biological bases of behavior

Cognition

Developmental psychology

History, approaches, and methods

Learning

Measurement and statistics

Motivation and emotion

Personality

Sensation and perception

Social psychology

State of consciousness

Treatment of psychological disorders

CLEP: INTRODUCTION TO EDUCATIONAL PSYCHOLOGY

RECOMMENDED READINGS

Educational Psychology: A Cognitive Approach, Mayer, 1987
Educational Psychology, Wollfolk, 4th ed., 1990
Educational Psychology, Principles and Applications, Glover and
 Bruning, 3rd ed., 1990

DESCRIPTION OF THE EXAMINATION

The introduction to educational psychology examination covers the material that is usually taught in a one-semester undergraduate course in this subject. Emphasis is placed on principles of learning and cognition, teaching methods and classroom management, child growth and development, and evaluation and assessment of learning.

KNOWLEDGE AND SKILLS REQUIRED (90 MINUTES)

1. Knowledge and comprehension of basic facts, concepts, and principles

2. Association of ideas with given theoretical positions

3. Awareness of important influences on learning and instruction

4. Familiarity with research and statistical concepts and procedures

5. Ability to apply various concepts and theories to particular teaching situations and problems

The subject matter of the introduction to educational psychology examination is drawn from the following topics:

Behavioristic perspectives

Cognitive perspective

Development

Educational aims and philosophies

Individual differences

Motivation

Pedagogy

Research design and analysis

Testing

PEP:RCE—FOUNDATIONS OF GERONTOLOGY

RECOMMENDED READINGS

Social Forces and Aging: An Introduction to Social Gerontology, 6th ed., R. C. Atchley, 1991

The Psychology of Aging: Theory, Research and Practice, 2nd ed., J. K. Belsky, 1990

Later Life: The Realities of Aging, 3rd ed., H. Cox, 1992

Social Gerontology, 3rd ed., N. R. Hooyman and H. A. Kiyak, 1993

The Realities of Aging: An Introduction to Gerontology, 3rd ed., C. Kart, 1990

The Economics of Aging, 5th ed., J. H. Schultz, 1992

Biology of Human Aging, A. Spence, 1989

DESCRIPTION OF THE EXAMINATION

This exam tests material typically taught in an introductory, one-semester course in gerontology. It measures knowledge and understanding of the biological, psychological, and social aspects of aging as well as the ability to describe, understand, and analyze issues, needs, and problems pertaining to the elderly and the aging process. The content covers theories, concepts, empirical patterns, and their implications for policy and procedure. The examination consists of multiple-choice questions and requires approximately three hours to complete.

KNOWLEDGE AND SKILLS REQUIRED

1. Knowledge of terminology, facts, and trends
2. Comprehension of major concepts, theories, and practices
3. The ability to analyze factors and variables operating in given situations

EXAMINATION BY CONTENT

Biology and Health

Death and Dying

Demography of Aging: Trends and Projections

Economics, Work, Retirement

Important Concepts of Gerontology

Political Behavior and Public Policy

Psychology and Mental Health

Sociology of Aging

Appendix B

Regents College
and
Thomas Edison State College

Regents College of the State University of New York, and Thomas Edison State College (TESC), a New Jersey state college, are two premier colleges that work with nontraditional adult students. Both will accept all credits in the form of testing if the degree requirements are met. And both colleges will work with associate's and bachelor's levels primarily through a variety of lifelong learning assessments. They have methods in common and each has some that are different. Both are excellent sources for ADs, using ASCs and *independent study* opportunities.

While you are deciding on your degree path and planning your educational directions, send for the catalogs from both colleges. They are easy to follow and very informative. Even if you do not select one of them as your college, you will learn many helpful short cuts that will aid you in developing an operational knowledge about the components of ADs. This knowledge of the components will provide you with an academic vocabulary, giving you the savvy to ask the right questions, no matter what college you check out.

REGENTS COLLEGE

Regents College was founded in 1970, and has over sixty thousand graduates. Not all of these graduates attained their degrees through testing, but all of them completed their undergraduate degrees without residency. Regents has no residency requirement of any kind. The only time you would be required to go to Regents is for academic assessment and challenge exams for *life credits*. Of course, you can voluntarily go there to attend your graduation (it's optional). Your diploma is mailed to you.

Testing Out and Assessment

Regents allows any student who chooses to use testing for all degrees that do not require a lab course or practice teaching. In some cases almost total testing is accepted, and special arrangements can be made for lab courses or practice teaching.

Assessment is provided if a student can go to Albany, New York. If you select this college and decide on assessment for life experience, you can achieve up to thirty credits per assessment session. In the history of Regents there have been only approximately twenty graduates who had high numbers of assessment credits awarded toward a degree, documenting their lifelong learning. This does not mean you cannot use this method to verify your college-level learning. It does mean that you should look at this realistically.

An assessment costs $975. It includes working with Regents College assessment staff to outline the requirements for the assessment to be conducted, including oral examinations. One group this process especially serves is musicians who can perform for their respective committees. In many cases, I feel that testing systems like the Graduate Record Exam, where a student can earn up to thirty credits for the cost of one test, offer more credits for the money.

The assessment process at Regents College encourages the use of testing systems to meet degree requirements rather the on site assessment. This is my philosophy as well. While you may have piles of papers from your life's work and lifelong learning, when a test matches the curriculum that is taught at colleges and reflects your learning it certainly constitutes the most credits for the least money. The inclusive nature of the test leaves no question as to whether your learning meets college-level criteria.

In my opinion, while assessments exist for nontraditional students, the conversations I have had with several academics still shows some uncertainty about assessment. However, even if testing still has a small number of academic detractors, even some who are openly skeptical, the fact is that a test is a test. A test has no gray areas. A recognized test score is hard proof of academic achievement.

Regents College Costs

All tests and courses are separate costs with respect to tuition and related fees. Regents costs as of September 1, 1995, are as follows:

Tuition/enrollment fee		$565.00
Annual advisement and evaluation fee		270.00*
Credit review fee		115.00
Program transfer fee		205.00†
Graduation fee	(bachelor's)	370.00
	(associate's)	340.00
Portfolio/academic assessment	(all levels)	$975.00

---

*This fee is charged every year until you graduate or drop out. For individuals who consider this fee an economic constraint, remember my suggestion for open student status until you are within a year of graduation.

†The program transfer fee covers transferring from one degree area to another, e.g., business to liberal arts.

Credit Review Fee

This $75 fee is a new process at Regents College. It is helpful for preenrollment considerations, and the $75 applies to your enrollment fee within three months of the evaluation. It's a small price to pay to be evaluated by a college, even if you decide not to complete a degree at Regents.

THOMAS EDISON STATE COLLEGE

Thomas Edison State College (TESC) was established in 1972, and has graduated over twelve thousand students. This is one of the rare colleges that will grant you *life credits* by assessing your lifelong learning and life experiences without credit limits, and you never have to leave your home area. With no residency requirement, the portfolio assessment can be accomplished at a distance, via mail, phone, and fax.

TESC Costs*

Tuition costs are in addition to any test fees or tuition and related expenses of coursework you take or have taken. Tuition costs at TESC as of July 1, 1995, are as follows:

---

*Always check the fee structure before you enroll.

	New Jersey Resident	Nonresident*
Application fee	$ 75	$ 75
Annual enrollment fee†	440	780
Annual enrollment fee international		1,000
Technology fee	30	30
Credit transfer evaluation fee		
1–5 credits	33	66
6–11	66	132
12–29	117	234
30–59	210	420
60–89	300	600
90–100	395	790
Graduation fee	125	125
TECEP, per exam attempted	40	60
Portfolio/practicum, per credit attempted	15	25
Guided study tuition		
Per credit attempted	51	76
Registration fee	$ 12	$ 12

---

*A nonresident student is one who maintains residence outside of the state of New Jersey or who is not a U.S. citizen and not a permanent resident of the United States.

†An enrolled student who wishes to remain active must pay the annual enrollment fee, due on the student's anniversary date. (Example: If you enroll on February 1, 1995, your annual enrollment fee [$420 or $780] would be due on February 1, 1996.)

CERTIFICATE PROGRAMS

In addition to degree programs listed in their catalogs, TESC provides opportunities for testing, portfolio assessment, guided study, and transfer credits. Certificates are available in the following professional areas:

Accounting	Labor Studies
Administrative Office	Management Marketing
Computer Aided Design	Management of Human Resources
Data Processing	Operations Management
Electronics	Public Administration
Finance	

GRADUATE SCHOOLS

Here is a partial listing of graduate schools that accept Regents College degrees based on the academic discipline of the graduate and undergraduate degree:*

American University	Arizona State University
Antioch University (Ohio)	Baylor University
Antioch University (Washington State)	Boston University
	Brigham Young University

*Regents College Alumni have prepared *Beyond Regents College*, a guide to graduate schools by state based on academic discipline, $6. If you plan or even have a distant dream to attend graduate school, this is a necessary resource.

Brooklyn Law School

Case Western Reserve
University

California State Universities

Columbia University

Cornell University

Embry-Riddle Aeronautical
University

Harvard University

Hunter College

John F. Kennedy University

Johns Hopkins University

Kent State University

Pepperdine University

Rochester Institute of
Technology

Rutgers University

State University of New York
(multiple locations)

Syracuse University

Pennsylvania State University

Trenton State University

University of Connecticut

University of Colorado

University of Florida

University of Hawaii

University of Kansas

University of Missouri

University of Oklahoma

University of Pennsylvania

University of Texas

University of Tulsa

University of Washington (state)

Yale University

Thomas Edison State College has the following partial list of college and universities that have accepted its graduates based on an alumni survey.

Alabama State University

American University

Antioch University

Atlanta Law School

Cleveland State University

Drew University

Fairleigh Dickinson University

Fielding Institute

Fordham University

Goucher College

Harvard University

Indiana University

Jersey City State College

Johns Hopkins University

John Jay College of Criminal Justice

Monmouth College

Montclair State College

Morgan State University

New York Institute of Technology

New York University

Ohio University

Pennsylvania State University

Princeton University

Rowan College of New Jersey

Rutgers University Law School

Syracuse University

Trenton State College

University of Toledo

Villanova Law School

OTHER COLLEGES THAT
ACCEPT INDEPENDENT STUDY

Here is a brief list of colleges offering accelerated degree programs that are based on the student's use of *independent study*, in whole or in part, requiring little or no residency.*

Brigham Young University
  Provo, Utah

California State University
  Dominquez Hills, Carson, California

College of Santa Fe
  Santa Fe, New Mexico

Columbia University, Teachers College
  New York City, New York

The Electronic University

Emoire State College
  Saratoga, New York

Evergreen State College
  Olympia, Washington

Loyola University
  New Orleans, Lousiana

New College, Saint Edward's University
  Austin, Texas.

Nova University
  Fort Lauderdale, Florida

---

*Thorson's Guide to Campus-Free Degrees, Marcie Kisner Thorson, Tulsa, Oklahoma, 1993.

Ohio University
    Athens, Ohio

Pennsylvania State University
    University Park, Pennsylvania

Rochester Institute of Technology
    Rochester, New York

State University of Florida External Degree Program
    Tampa, Florida

Syracuse University
    Syracuse, New York

University of Oklahoma
    Norman, Oklahoma

Appendix C

Mini-Quiz[*]

Academic Preparation and Assessment

Find out if you are a good candidate for an undergraduate degree using *independent study*. Take this mini quiz to determine how well an *independent study* course would fit your circumstances and lifestyle? *Write the letter of your answer to each question on a piece of paper and score as directed.*

1. My need to take this course now is:

   a. High—I need it immediately for degree, job, or other reason.

   b. Moderate—I could take it later or substitute another course.

   c. Low—It's a personal interest that could be postponed.

---

*Erie Community College North (SUNY), Buffalo, New York. Found in Telecourse booklet, pp. 3–4. It has been adapted to quiz you on *independent study* and your educational goals. Originally taken from the *PBS Adult Learning Service Newsletter* 9: 1 (Spring 1994), with instructions that state, "Feel free to reproduce."

2. Feeling that I am part of a class is:

    a. Not particularly necessary to me.

    b. Somewhat important to me.

    c. Very important to me.

3. I would classify myself as someone who:

    a. Often gets things done ahead of time.

    b. Needs reminding to get things done on time.

    c. Puts things off until the last minute.

4. Classroom discussion is:

    a. Rarely helpful to me.

    b. Sometimes helpful to me.

    c. Almost always helpful to me.

5. When an instructor hands out directions for an assignment I prefer:

    a. Figuring out the instructions myself.

    b. Trying to follow instruction on my own, then asking for help as needed.

    c. Having the instructions explained to me.

6. I need faculty comments on my assignments:

    a. Within a few weeks, so that I can review what I did (in some cases, not at all).

    b. Within a few days, or I forget what I did.

    c. Right away, or I get frustrated.

7. Considering my professional and personal schedule, the amount of time I have to work on an *independent study* is:

    a. More than enough for a campus class or an *independent study* course.

    b. The same as it would be for a class or an *independent study* course.

    c. Less than for a class on campus.

8. When I am asked to use VCRs, computers voice mail, or other technologies new to me:

    a. I look forward to learning new skills.

    b. I feel apprehensive, but try anyway.

    c. I put it off or try to avoid it.

9. As a reader, I would classify myself as:

    a. Good—I usually understand.

    b. Average—I sometimes need help to understand course materials.

    c. Slower than average.

10. If I have to go to campus to take exams or complete work:

    a. I can go to campus anytime.

    b. I may miss some lab assignments or exam deadlines if campus labs are not open evenings and weekends.

    c. I will have difficulty getting to campus, even in the evening and on weekends.

Scoring

Add three points for each "a" that you circled, two for each "b," and one for each "c."

a. _____   b. _____   c. _____   Total _____

A score of 20 or more means *independent study* is a real possibility for you.

A score between 11 and 20 means *independent study* is a possibility for you with some preparation.

A score of 10 or less means *independent study* may not currently be the best alternative for you.

Explanations

The ten questions above reflect some of the facts about using *independent study*.

1. *Independent study* students can sometimes end up neglecting their studies because of personal or professional circumstances, unless they have compelling reasons to study this way.

2. Some students prefer the independence of *independent study*, others find it uncomfortable.

3. *Independent study* gives students greater freedom of scheduling, but it can require more self-discipline than on-campus classes.

4. Some students learn best by interacting with other students and instructors, but *independent study* often does not provide much opportunity for this interaction.

5. *Independent study* requires you to work from written directions without face-to-face instructions, or in some cases, like *testing*, without feedback while you are learning.

6. *Independent study* coursework has a longer response (feedback) time from instructors using the mail. Feedback from testing happens when your final test score is sent to you.

7. *Independent study* courses require almost the same amount of actual learning time, without classroom time and related expenses.

8. *Independent study* frequently uses technology for teaching and communications.

9. Print materials are the primary source of directions and information in *independent study*.

10. All *independent study* requires some on-campus work, exams, library resources, and related activities.

Appendix D

College Check List

When considering a college for possible degree completion, use this check list to weight the items that are most important to you. Put pluses (+) by those items. When you complete the check list for each college, those with the most pluses (+) filled in should be the first colleges you consider and look at in more depth for your degree planning.

_____ Is the college accredited?

_____ What programs are available in your area of interest?

_____ Is the degree program or coursework accepted at schools you plan to attend in the future?

_____ What are the admissions requirements?

_____ Are they reachable?

_____ Are entrance tests required for admissions (e.g., SAT, ACT, or the school's particular entrance exam)?

_____ What are the tuition costs?

_____ Is financial aid and/or scholarship money available?

_____ How much?

_____ From what sources?

_____ What previous coursework can be transferred and accepted?

_____ What do books cost?

_____ Are there one-time registration and student activity fees?

_____ Are there lab fees and/or course supply costs?

_____ What expenses must be budgeted for: travel, parking, meals, and room and board?

_____ What are deadlines for financial aid and scholarships?

_____ How long will it take to complete the degree full-time/part-time?

_____ Will the college process and grant credits for "life experience"?

_____ What is the cost for processing transfer and "life experience" credits?

_____ What is the residency requirement, if any?

_____ How flexible is the class or course scheduling?

_____ Is commuting required?

     _____ How far?

     _____ At what cost?

_____ Is distance travel required?

     _____ How far?

     _____ At what cost?

_____ What is the reputation of the school relative to your chosen career (remember, "academic currency")?

_____ What is the local and national reputation of the college (remember, local and national hiring preferences)?

_____ If needed, does the college provide counseling with career development?

_____ If refresher or basic skills courses/workshops are needed, are they available (remember, "academic preparedness")?

_____ If on-campus courses are used, does the campus have child care?

     _____ Housing (when necessary)?

     _____ On-campus parking/transportation?

Books You Should Read

(Titles are listed in their order of importance for immediate reference.)

But first . . .

Distance Learn. Computers have arrived! This is a database available at most public libraries. The content allows for a degree search of colleges that provide distance degrees from associate's through the doctorate, and it's usually free to the public. According to the Peter C. Cornell Lifelong Learning Center at the Buffalo and Erie County Public Library, Buffalo, New York, you can search for colleges according to the degree level and subject area. The data include degree and residency requirements.

Council for Adult and Experiential Learning (CAEL), Chicago, Ill., 223 West Jackson Boulevard, Suite 510, Chicago, IL 60606, provides a comprehensive book titled *Earn College Credit for What You Know,*

2nd edition, Lois Lamdin, 1992, $21.50, $5 S&H, MC/Visa accepted. This book helps you evaluate your academic preparedness by doing the "Then & Now" exercise (p. 5), a "Consumer's Guide" section (p. 43), has excellent information in its portfolio assessment section (pp. 83–133), a list of generally accepted certificates and licenses (p. 176), and a comprehensive, state-by-state list of colleges that have programs that assess prior learning (pp. 195–241). Overall this is an excellent idea and reference book—a must read. (Susan Simisko authored the 1985 edition of this book for CAEL. If the Lamdin edition is unavailable, the Simisko edition is likely to be in most public libraries.)

Portfolio Development in Adult Learning: Purposes and Strategies, Alan Mandell. This is another CAEL publication of interest: $21.50, $5 S&H, MC/Visa accepted.

One Year to a College Degree, Lynette Long and Eileen Hershberger, Lafayette, La.: Huntington House Publishers, 1992. This is an excellent book and a must read. Like me, Eileen Hershberger lived the process. She and Dr. Long describe her "how to" tips for campus attendance. While this information is tied to a campus degree, it covers many lifelong learning suggestions on the use of accredited short cuts in addition to taking campus classes. This book will help those of you who are bound by professional requirements to secure the maximum amount of credits to complete a degree in your own community. This is another good book to stimulate your ideas.

Guide to Educational Credit by Examination, Joan Schwartz (ed.), American Council on Education (ACE), One Du Pont Circle, Washington, DC 20036, 1992. The next edition is due out January 1996 at $27.50 (includes shipping and handling). This is a "must see" guidebook to testing systems. It covers content, suggested credits, and required test scores. It should be available at your local library.

Peterson's Guides provide numerous publications that assist the adult learner. Most Peterson's Guide publications recommended in this book are in your public library. However, the Peterson's Guides catalog is available by calling 800–338–3282. Getting on the company's mailing list is helpful, since you will receive its updated catalog for several mailings. Two guides that Peterson's has published in the 1980s and 1990s could be very helpful to you:

New Horizons: The Education and Career Planning Guide for Adults, William Haponski and Charles McCabe, Princeton, N.J., 1992 (possibly out of print). Available at most public libraries. Most library copies are copyrighted 1985. It is an excellent book on study planning for optimum learning and has extensive coverage of departmental exams. This book is to college degree completion what *What Color Is Your Parachute* (see listing below) is to a job search.

Independent Study Catalog: The NUCEA Guide to Continuing Education Through Correspondence Courses, 5th edition, Princeton, N.J.: 1994–95. This guidebook has a listing of the top seventy-two correspondence colleges including the University of Kansas, Ohio University, Pennsylvania State University, and Syracuse University, to name a few. Available at most public library systems, or order from Peterson's Guides at 800–338–3282. $16.95, plus $5.75 S&H, MC/Visa accepted. This reference book lists all the courses available at each of these top colleges and universities. From these lists you can send for the free college catalogs to secure detailed course descriptions. These descriptions will provide information for taking courses, and they can assist you in *life credits* assessments.

Thorson's Guide, 7th edition, Marcie Kisner Thorson, Tulsa, Okla., 1995. The 1992 edition is available at most public libraries. However, the 1995 edition has so many more AD/ASC schools to consider, if you are serious you might want to order your own copy by calling 918–622–2811. The price is $19.95, $5 S&H. Fax orders, 918–622–2811, MC/Visa accepted.

Regents College catalogs, 7 Columbia Circle, Albany, N.Y. 12203–5159, call 518–464–8500, Fax 518–464–8777.

Thomas Edison College catalogs, Thomas Edison State College, 101 West State Street, Trenton, N.J., 08608–1176, 609–984–1105, Fax 609–989–9321.

NOTE: Both Regents College and Thomas Edison State College catalogs are excellent resources, even if you select another college.

How to Earn a College Degree Without Going to College, James Duffy, New York: John Wiley & Sons, 1992. This book has an excellent section on *independent study* (pages 25–47) and a comprehensive section on colleges offering distance/external degrees (pages 49–66). This is one of the few books that have such a comprehensive list by academic/career categories.

The Electronic University, 1977 Colestin Road, Hornbrook, CA 96044, call 800–22LEARN. This system of distance learning provides all degree levels accessible by computer, from the associate's through the doctorate. The university provides a free video covering its programs, and has software that gives you a free mini-course to see if you would have an interest in completing a degree or doing coursework through the university's system. This system of degrees, totally by computer, has quadrupled its services since the mid-1980s when I first evaluated it.

Adult Learners Survival Skills, Bill Bittel, Melbourne, Fla.: Krieger Publishing Company, Inc., 1990. A valuable booklet that can help you jump start both your attitude and ability to succeed at college.

Ace Any Test: Ron Fry's How to Study Program, Ron Fry, Franklin Lakes, N.J.: Career Press, Inc., 1994. Other study guide books by Ron Fry are at most public libraries and book stores. His series on "how to" study, take exams, and take notes, and more is worth the time, and can help you plan for college and succeed once there.

Additional Reading

Smart Choices: A Woman's Guide to Returning to College, Anne Bianchi, Princeton, N.J.: Peterson's Guides, 1990. This is another book that should be in your local library. It's well worth reviewing.

The Electronic University: A Guide to Distance Learning Programs, Princeton, N.J.: Peterson's Guides, 1993, or call 800–338–3282. Available at most libraries. As with any book that covers distance education, it is valuable to review the suggestions in this book regarding computer-generated learning.

What Color Is Your Parachute? Richard Nelson Bolles, Berkeley, Calif.: Ten Speed Press, 1994. This book is very helpful in career planning and learning about hiring practices. It is annually updated, but any copy with a 1990 copyright or newer would be helpful. Available at most libraries.

Career Fitness: How to Find, Win, and Keep the Job You Want in the 1990s, Peter D. Weddle, New York: Cadell and Davis, 1994. This book helps you determine what you need to do to prepare for success in your chosen career.

Unicorns Are Real. Barbara Meister Vitale, Torrance, Calif.: Jalmar Press, 1982. This book was written by an elementary teacher for elementary teachers. Enlightening for those adults who have learning deficits, it's worth a quick review to help you see what your best learning style is and to gather some tips on helping yourself learn with both the right and left sides of your brain. Available at most libraries.

Testing Systems Addresses

(Listed in Alphabetical Order)

American College Testing Proficiency Exam Program: Regents College Examinations—PEP:RCE

ACT PEP:RCE
P.O. Box 168
Iowa City, IA 52243

American Payroll Association

American Payroll Association
30 E. 33rd, 5th Floor
New York, NY 10016

Cardiovascular Credentialing International (CCI)

CCI/NBCVT
P.O. Box 611
Wright Brothers Station
Dayton, Ohio 45409–0611

College-Level Exam Program—CLEP

CLEP—College-Level Examination Program
Educational Testing Service
Princeton, NJ 08541

or

CLEP Program Services Officer
The College Board
45 Columbus Avenue
New York, NY 10023–6917

DANTES—Defense Activity for Non-Traditional Education Support

DANTES Examination/Certification Division
Saufley Field
Pensacola, FL 32509–7400

Defense Language Proficiency Test (DLPT)

The Commandant
The Defense Language Institute
Foreign Language Center
The Presidio of Monterey
Monterey, CA 93944–5006

ATTN: ATFL-EST

Foreign Service Institute

Testing Unit Head
School of Language Studies
Foreign Service Institute
1400 Key Blvd., Suite 900
Arlington, VA 22209

Learningforce, Inc.

College Courses by Video—Credit by Examination
1027 33rd Street, NW
Washington, DC 20007

Call: 800–852–5277

New York University Proficiency Testing in Foreign Language

Foreign Language Program, NYU
School of Continuing Education
48 Cooper Square, Room 107
New York, NY 10003

Ohio University Course Credit by Examination (CCE)

Ohio University CCE
Lifelong Learning Programs
302 Tupper Hall
Ohio University
Athens, Ohio 45701–2979

Phone: 800–444–2910

Professional Secretaries International
(formerly National Secretaries Association)

Professional Secretaries International
CPS Division
301 East Armour Blvd.
Kansas City, MO 64111–1299

The National Computing Centre (NCC)

The National Computing Centre
Oxford Rd.
Manchester
England M1 7ED

National Court Reporters Association (NCRA)

National Court Reporters Association
8224 Old Court House Rd.
Vienna, VA 22182–3808

The National Institute for Automotive Service Excellence (ASE)

National Institute for Automotive Service Excellence
13505 Dulles Technology Drive
Herndon, VA 22071-3415

Accreditation Agencies

As stated in *Thorson's Campus-Free Degrees:**

At times literature from various *unaccredited* schools contain terminology designed to mislead the public. Beware of official-sounding phrases such as "we are pursuing accreditation," "registered," and "member of _____." Some unaccredited schools actually use the term "accredited by" followed by the name of an "accrediting agency" which in truth they themselves have set up with the specific intention of deceiving the public. If you're unsure about the status of any institution, check with the recognized authorities listed below.

---

*Thorson's Guide to Campus-Free Degrees, 6th edition, Tulsa, Okla.: 1994, pp. 7–19, has in-depth information on accreditation, including vocational accreditation agencies.

1. Commission of Higher Education
   Middle States Association of Colleges and Schools
   3624 Market Street
   Philadelphia, PA 19104

   215–662–5606.

   The following states, districts, and territories report here: Delaware, District of Columbia, Maryland, New Jersey, New York, Pennsylvania, Puerto Rico, Virgin Islands.

2. Commission of Institutions of Higher Education
   New England Association of Schools and Colleges
   Sanborn House
   15 High Street
   Winchester, MA 01890

   617–729–6762.

   The following states report here: Connecticut, Maine, New Hampshire, Rhode Island, Vermont.

3. Commission on Institutions of Higher Education
   North Central Association of Colleges and Schools
   159 North Dearborn
   Chicago, IL 60601

   312–263–0456.

   The following states report here: Arizona, Arkansas, Colorado, Illinois, Indiana, Iowa, Kansas, Michigan, Minnesota, Missouri, Nebraska, New Mexico, North Dakota, Ohio, Oklahoma, South Dakota, West Virginia, Wisconsin, Wyoming.

4. Commission on Colleges
   Northwest Association of Schools and Colleges
   3700–B University Way, NE
   Seattle, WA 98105

   206–543–0195.

   The following states report here: Alaska, Idaho, Montana, Nevada, Oregon, Utah, Washington.

5. Commission on Colleges
   Southern Association of Colleges and Schools
   1866 Southern Lane
   Decatur, GA 30033

   404–329–6500 or 800–248–7701.

   The following states report here: Alabama, Florida, Georgia, Kentucky, Louisiana, Mississippi, North Carolina, South Carolina, Tennessee, Texas, Virginia.

6. Accrediting Commission for Senior Colleges and Universities
   Western Association of Schools and Colleges
   Mills College
   Box 9990
   Oakland, CA 94613

   415–632–5000.

   The following states and territories report here: California, Hawaii, American Samoa, Guam, and the Commonwealth of the Northern Marianas.

Terms You Need to Know

Accelerated degree (AD): an undergraduate degree path, whether traditional or nontraditional, that facilitates the student in completing a degree without a traditional course-by-course approach, but instead provides more flexible learning methods, e.g., one class per week, credit for life experiences, and others. Accelerated undergraduate degrees have a delivery system that provides degree completion through learning methods that speed up course work or related learning for adults over the age of twenty-five. *See* distance, extension, external, off-campus, and outreach degrees.

Accredited degree: a degree granted from a college that is accredited by one of the six primary accrediting agencies.

Accredited short cut (ASC): the accredited learning methods that a student can use to complete an undergraduate degree without classroom attendance.

Adult student: a student over the age of twenty-five who has returned to college after a minimum of a year of not participating in any formal education.

Approved degree: a degree granted by a college that is academically approved by its state, or by an agency it has chosen, but not accredited by the six major accreditation agencies that are nationally and internationally accepted for accreditation.

Associate's degree: a degree that requires 60 semester credits, or 90 quarter credits, of subjects designated by a college.

Bachelor's degree: a degree that requires 120 semester credits, or 180 quarter credits, of subjects designated by a college.

College (university): an institution of higher education that grants a college degree. In this book "college" refers to both.

Computer-generated degrees/courses: degree-related courses delivered by computer accompanied by textbooks and a syllabus (e.g., the Electronic University).

Continuing Education Units (CEUs): programs generated by colleges for students who need to maintain licensure, e.g., nurses and teachers. The number of applicable credits varies depending upon the program accepting them.

Coursework: the study and learning achieved through formal, structured curriculum parameters set up by a school. In this book the term will refer to college-equivalent learning.

Degree: the credential granted on completion of required coursework at a college or university.

Degree requirements: the coursework and semester or quarter credits that each college determines constitutes the content of a particular degree that it confers.

Diploma mill: a business that is neither an accredited nor an approved college. It charges a fee to produce a transcript and diploma that appears legitimate, but is not.

Distance degree: a degree obtained from a college that is not in your community, but provides a degree program that you can complete wherever you live. *See* extension, external, off-campus, and outreach degrees.

Doctorate degree: a graduate degree beyond the master's degree, requiring 60 to 90 semester credits or 90 to 135 quarter credits. The most widely known doctorates are the Ph.D., the Ed.D., and the J.D. A Ph.D. is a doctor of philosophy, which means a substantial research project was completed in addition to graduate-level coursework. An Ed.D. is a doctor of education, and can mean either teaching or research was completed in addition to graduate level coursework (usually the research is not as in-depth and comprehensive as that completed for a Ph.D., but this depends on the college where the Ed.D. is conferred). A J.D. is a doctor of law from a law school.

Experiential learning: learning through life experiences—an ongoing process of lifelong learning from formal and informal sources other than the learning generated from a college.

External degree: a degree completed off campus. It can be earned at an outreach campus away from a college's main campus that sponsors the degree. In either case, the same degree requirements must be fulfilled. *See* distance, extension, off-campus, and outreach degrees.

Independent study: a way of completing college coursework on one's own, separate from the classroom. Students taking independent study courses must demonstrate a command of the subject matter through testing or other means agreed upon by the student and the college or organization sponsoring the learning.

Interactive courses: students at several locations interact by television or telephone with the professor and the students at some central location and with students at other outreach or extension sites. *See* telenet course and television courses.

Learning contract (study plan): a learning agreement or document designed by the student and implemented between the student and the college to cover the learning objectives, content, and outcome for a college course or degree.

Learning preference: the desired circumstances in which an individual finds learning comfortable, e.g., bright light versus dim light, noise versus quiet.

Learning style: the manner in which an individual seems best able to learn, e.g., independently or in a classroom.

Life credits: credits granted within a degree program for lifelong learning accomplished through life experiences (experiential learning), and validated through a portfolio assessment.

Lifelong learning (experiential learning): a process beginning at birth and continuing throughout adulthood from both formal and informal sources.

Master's degree: a graduate degree that requires 30 to 36 semester credits, or 45 to 54 quarter credits. Master's coursework usually focuses on a specific field.

No residency: a student can meet degree requirements by taking courses from multiple sources without taking any classes from the college that will grant a degree for this work.

Non-collegiate learning: learning from all sources other than a college, e.g., business and industry training, professional seminars, vocational training, and the like.

Off-campus degree: a distance, external, or outreach degree depending on the college offering it and the location of the delivery of the degree. This degree usually has the same requirements as the campus degree program that sponsors it. *See* distance, extension, external, and outreach degrees.

Outreach and extension courses: any collegiate, noncollegiate, or vocational learning generated from a central educational location. The same textbooks and syllabus are used at all locations.

Outreach degree: a degree provided by a college at an outreach location, separate from the main campus. This degree usually has the same requirements as the campus degree program that sponsors it. *See* distance, extension, external, and off-campus degrees.

Portfolio assessment: the methods designated by a college to grant credits for lifelong and experiential learning in campus, off-campus, traditional, nontraditional, and accelerated degrees.

Quarter credit hours: a standard measurement for college credits that applies to some college-generated courses. A 4.5 quarter credit course is equivalent to a 3 semester credit course. One semester credit is equal to 1.5 quarter credits.

Residency: the number of required credit courses from a college in order to grant a degree from that college. This requires the student to attend campus classes or complete coursework off campus directly from the college granting the degree.

Semester credit hours: a standard measurement for college credits that apply to each college-generated course. The usual amount of semester credit hours granted for a single course is 3 and 6.

Study plan (learning agreement): the independent study coursework (for a specified timeframe or to meet degree requirements) that is outlined and agreed to by a college and a student. Most study plans are used for accelerated and off-campus degrees. Study plans that outline an entire degree program are sometimes considered the same as learning contracts.

Teaching style: the method of education delivery, e.g., lecture, audio, video, independent study.

Telenet course: a course that is generated from a central facility over telephone lines to outreach and extension sites, usually statewide, using the same textbooks and syllabus as the campus course.

Television course: a course presented on television, e.g., Mind Extension University on cable television.

Video/audio courses: courses with guided study presented on video/audio tapes with the help of textbooks and a syllabus.

Index

DATE DUE
